The Birmingham Good Friday march, on April 12, 1963, led by (from left) Fred Shuttlesworth, Ralph Abernathy and Martin Luther King Jr.
(Used by permission of Birmingham, Alabama, Public Library Archives.)

"We remember Martin Luther King Jr. because he spoke truth to power. We remember Dr. King because he cast a vision for what we could be, rather than what we often are. Now, Edward Gilbreath uses historical insight, theological sensitivity and nitty-gritty honesty to help us remember King for his challenges to the church. If you want your congregation to be and remain on the side of justice, you will get a copy of *Birmingham Revolution* for your pastor. If you want it to change your life, you'll get another one for yourself."

Edward J. Blum, coauthor of *The Color of Christ*

"Ed Gilbreath offers a masterful retelling of key times in the life of King. He gives us a holistic view that helps us to understand the great civil rights leader. Gilbreath does not sidestep controversial issues so that we will engage in an unspiritual worship of King but places the man in a proper context so that we gain qualitative insight into the civil rights movement."

George Yancey, professor of sociology, University of North Texas

"Edward Gilbreath has written a smart, thoughtful and contemporary account of Martin Luther King Jr.'s 'Letter from a Birmingham Jail.' He analyzes the depth of King's theological convictions concerning racial injustices and the controversies they provoked in the city of Birmingham in 1963, as well as the nation. Gilbreath's book prophetically challenges evangelical Christians to reexamine King's theological convictions in light of racial and social class inequities facing the United States and the world today."

Randal Maurice Jelks, author of Benjamin Elijah Mays, *Schoolmaster of the Movement*

"Today, the historical significance of Dr. Martin Luther King has either been virtually forgotten or has given way to a slew of one-dimensional caricatures. In *Birmingham Revolution*, Ed Gilbreath not only gives a fresh analysis of an important chapter of the civil rights movement, he also thoughtfully reintroduces Dr. King to a whole new generation. He challenges us to reexamine Dr. King's renowned 'Letter from a Birmingham Jail' in order to rediscover the clear biblical concerns and mandates for justice. This book will prove to be a valuable tool in equipping those we disciple with a fuller application of God's Word in the cultural marketplace."

Carl Ellis Jr., assistant professor of practical theology, Redeemer Seminary

"This book offers a unique facet to the multifaceted jewel of Martin Luther King Jr. and the Birmingham revolution. The one who dares to take another look into the life, work and ministry of King by reading this book will experience the transition from a glimpse to a glance to a glaze."

Robert Smith Jr., professor of divinity, Beeson Divinity School, Birmingham, Alabama

BIRMINGHAM REVOLUTION

MARTIN LUTHER KING JR.'S
EPIC CHALLENGE TO THE CHURCH

EDWARD GILBREATH

IVP Books

An imprint of InterVarsity Press
Downers Grove, Illinois

InterVarsity Press
P.O. Box 1400, Downers Grove, IL 60515-1426
World Wide Web: www.ivpress.com
Email: email@ivpress.com

InterVarsity Press® is the book-publishing division of InterVarsity Christian Fellowship/USA®, a movement of students and faculty active on campus at hundreds of universities, colleges and schools of nursing in the United States of America, and a member movement of the International Fellowship of Evangelical Students. For information about local and regional activities, write Public Relations Dept., InterVarsity Christian Fellowship/USA, 6400 Schroeder Rd., P.O. Box 7895, Madison, WI 53707-7895, or visit the IVCF website at www.intervarsity.org.

While all stories in this book are true, some names and identifying information in this book have been changed to protect the privacy of the individuals involved.

Design: Cindy Kiple
Images: The March on Birmingham: The Granger Collection, NYC/ All rights reserved.
  Dr. Martin Luther King Jr.: The Granger Collection, NYC/ All rights reserved.
  Photo of Edward Gilbreath: Phil Marcelo

ISBN 978-0-8308-3769-4 (print)
ISBN 978-0-8308-8445-2 (digital)

Printed in the United States of America ∞

Library of Congress Cataloging-in-Publication Data
A catalog record for this book is available from the Library of Congress.

P	18	17	16	15	14	13	12	11	10	9	8	7	6	5	4	3	2	1
Y	28	27	26	25	24	23	22	21	20	19	18	17	16	15	14	13

CONTENTS

Prologue: *King's Wittenberg Moment* 9

1 Birmingham Begins 19

2 The Making of Martin 31

3 Montgomery Miracle 42

4 The Road to Revolution 54

5 As Birmingham Goes 63

6 Eight White Preachers,
   or With Friends Like These 72

7 An Angry Dr. King 88

8 The Jailhouse Manifesto 98

9 "My Dear Fellow Clergymen" 106

10 Taking It to the Streets 119

11 Dreams and Nightmares 135

12 After the Revolution 146

13 King Among the Evangelicals 156

Epilogue: *King's Epistle for Today* 164

Acknowledgments 171

Notes 175

Recommended Reading on Race,
MLK and the Civil Rights Movement   198

Index   203

About the Author   208

For my loving wife, Dana
And for the children of the revolution

Martin has used the Negro church as a kind of tool
not only to liberate Negroes, but to liberate the entire country.
The only people in the country at the moment who even believe
in Christianity are the most despised minority in it.

JAMES BALDWIN

✠

History throws a light on it.
We are in a revolutionary situation,
and all through history it's the despised minorities
—the proletarians, the peasants, the poor—
who recaptured the heights
and depths of faith.

REINHOLD NIEBUHR

✠

from *The Meaning of the Birmingham Tragedy,* September 22, 1963

KING'S WITTENBERG MOMENT

*Here I stand; I cannot do
otherwise, so help me God.*

MARTIN LUTHER

*I am in Birmingham
because injustice is here.*

MARTIN LUTHER KING JR.

MARTIN LUTHER WAS ON A MISSION to restore righteousness to the church. On October 31, 1517, when the Catholic monk and scholar hammered his list of ninety-five theological arguments to the front door of All Saints' Church in Wittenberg, Germany, he helped usher in a new era of Christian activism—of speaking truth to power. In Luther's day the medieval church's papal hierarchy had become so rich, greedy and political that its moral authority sank. Luther's Ninety-Five Theses was a principled stand against hypocrisy and side hustles. He wanted to reform the church from the inside out. Thanks to the Gutenberg press—his era's digital media—Luther's blistering critique soon went viral, circulating as pamphlets throughout Europe and stirring questions in the minds of others who were disturbed by the Church's corruption. Luther was a flawed hero whose legacy is debated to this day, but his actions signaled the opening salvo of a revolution.

Four hundred years later, another Martin Luther sparked an equally revolutionary uprising in the United States. Starting in Montgomery, Alabama, in 1955 and spreading outward, Martin Luther King Jr. upset the Southern social order of racial segregation and white supremacy by boldly reappropriating a simple American idea: "We hold these truths to be self-evident, that all men are created equal."

As an African American kid growing up in the Midwest in the 1970s, I always viewed Martin Luther King Jr. as a fantastical sort of figure—an American folk hero who could give a good speech. On the "Cool Black Persons Index," he fell somewhere between John Henry and Muhammad Ali. Then I went to high school in the 1980s and learned more about the stuff that came before and after his signature "I Have a Dream" moment—the buses and bombs, police dogs and fire hoses. In time King became a bit more real to me, like a dead poet or pioneering inventor. In the 1990s I attended a Christian college and went on to work for an evangelical magazine. I soon discovered that racial tension and division were alive and well in American Christianity. In what would become an ongoing quest to understand it all, I returned to King. Among his many works, I read his "Letter from Birmingham Jail." Suddenly, King became a prophet.

THE STRANGE AND TRAGIC IDEA OF RACE IN AMERICA

When Martin Luther King Jr. arrived on the national scene in the late 1950s, America was at a point somewhat similar to where we are today in regard to race: though there had been significant political breakthroughs that signaled racial progress (e.g., *Brown v. the Board of Education* then, the election of President Barack Obama today), the reality on the ground was a completely different story. In both cases, people of color risked offending white people if they dared broach the subject of race.

Of course, there are big differences. Back in the day, "Negroes" were simply expected to know their place in society as the inferior race and to accept it. Today the feeling among many white Americans is that people of color, and particularly African Americans, should be satisfied with the tremendous advances in race relations since the civil rights period, and that to bring up perceived inequalities is to expose oneself as either a whiner or a race baiter.

Race, as both a social construct and a visible reality, is the gigantic elephant in the American living room that some insist will disappear if only we would just ignore it. For African Americans and other people of color, however, it is difficult to ignore a six-ton pachyderm when it's sitting on top of you.

In 1910, W. E. B. Du Bois observed how odd the notion of race is in the context of larger human history. "The discovery of personal whiteness among the world's peoples," he said, "is a very modern thing." He added that the "ancient world would have laughed at such a distinction" and that in the Middle Ages skin color would have provoked nothing more than "mild curiosity." For the most part, Du Bois was correct. To be sure, early Europeans did recognize differences between their skin color and that of non-Europeans; however, the concept of "personal whiteness"—the idea that it could be owned as an asset and as a symbol of identity—was yet to come. As late as the seventeenth century, privileged male Europeans did not think of themselves as physically white, and the notion of "white" as a noun was unheard of. The concept of race grew once white Europeans discovered usefulness in equating their fair complexion with their possession of power. As they learned to exert that power to their advantage, they imposed a stigma of weakness and inferiority on those of a darker complexion.

Today, of course, the idea of race is so entrenched in our thinking that it's almost impossible to imagine not seeing the world through a *racialized* lens. This is especially true for the United States, a nation that emerged with a bang from the bold idea that "all men are created equal" but was thrust into a bloody civil war less than a century later over the question of whether some men should be treated unequally because of their skin color.

Variations on themes of freedom, equality and justice have infused almost every social and political issue since. And race has been right there alongside them, like a pesky cough from years of chain smoking. Even those who claim to be colorblind when it comes to matters of racial difference do so out of a tacit impulse to absolve themselves of what early civil rights leaders Frederick Douglass, Booker T. Washington and Du Bois famously called "the race problem."

But what many in our nation persistently overlook or deny, to our collective peril, is the fact that we're each complicit in the problem, and we each have a role to play in resolving it. The reasons for this are both historical and theological. Historical because our past ideas and actions have consequences; theological because both people and nations invariably reap what they sow.

There are at least two race-related facts about our nation's founding that we cannot get around. First, Native Americans, the original inhabitants of the territory that eventually would become the United States, were usurped from the land by a combination of force and political deceit. "Our nation was born in genocide when it embraced the doctrine that the original American, the Indian, was an inferior race," said Martin Luther King Jr. in 1964. "Even before there were large numbers of Negroes on our shores, the scar of racial hatred had already disfigured colonial society."

But there's a second troubling detail related to our nation's founding. For the first eighty-nine years of its official existence, the United States was a nation whose growth and prosperity was dependent on African and African American slave labor. Though chattel slavery had been legal in the American colonies for over a century before the 1776 birth of our nation, it was at first a mostly economic idea. The conflation of race with societal status was a gradual occurrence inherited from the colonists' European roots. Still, the idea would become so ingrained in the white psyche that it would permeate even the nation's understanding of Christianity. In time it became clear that both a political and spiritual transformation would be necessary to dislodge the nation's dependence on slavery and its anxieties about race. Warfare, regrettably, became the vehicle for solving this quandary.

Though the Civil War and President Lincoln's 1863 signing of the Emancipation Proclamation would lead to the end of American slavery, restoring the Confederate States to the Union and finding resolution on the dilemma of race would prove to be more problematic. Reconstruction, America's first experiment in interracial democracy, marked a brief period of promise for integrationists. But like a shooting star it quickly flamed out, imploding under the twin pressures of white hostility and fear. By 1876 the Southern states had installed a new brand of racial oppression through a vigorously enforced caste system named after a nineteenth-century minstrel character. These "Jim Crow" laws reversed many of the Constitutional rights that had been granted to African Americans after the Civil War and served to rigidly—and often violently—segregate blacks from whites. Consequently, each legislative advance for black Americans would be met with a hostile pushback from segregationists. *Brown v. the Board of Education*, in 1954, and the subsequent forced desegregation of public schools would lead to fortified efforts of racial discrimination in commerce and other areas of daily life; the Civil Rights Act of 1964 would lead to increased determinations to hinder black citizens from their right to vote; the 1965 Voting Rights Act would give way to bigger inequalities in employment and housing; affirmative action laws initiated in the 1970s continue to spark ideological chatter and resentment. And on it goes.

Even today, whether it's in debates about immigration, economic redistribution or presidential birth certificates, race continues to provoke in us angry and irrational reactions that you'd think we would have purged ourselves of long ago. The Christian understanding of human behavior, and its proclivity for sin, explains our continued struggle with matters of racism and discrimination. But that awareness in and of itself has not given American Christians any discernible measure of advantage in overcoming racial obstacles.

Nonetheless, from time to time prophetic Christian voices rise in timbre to challenge our nation's "original sin." In the nineteenth century the antislavery movement was filled with such voices. In the twentieth century, compelled by the Spirit of God and a yearning for freedom, the African American church took the lead in heralding the effort. Like almost no other movement before or since, Christian people gave force to a social mission designed to expose and ultimately dismantle an unjust American system. And, remarkably, they did it largely through nonviolent actions. Dr. Martin Luther King Jr.'s words and historic efforts as the Moses of this civil rights movement stands out as perhaps the most significant instance of a modern Christian leader acting in a prophetic role to instigate political change.

OCCUPYING THE BELOVED COMMUNITY

Part of the genius of Martin Luther King Jr. was his ability to interpret America's racial crisis and provide a nation newly rooted in the television age with vivid illustrations of what racial injustice and inhumanity looked like. But he didn't stop there. He also worked to supply a hopeful picture of where we could go, a sort of travel brochure for what he called "the beloved community"—an integrated America that values justice, reconciliation and peace. "But the end is reconciliation," King said in 1956 following the successful completion of the Montgomery bus protest, "the end is redemption; the end is the creation of the beloved community." He continued:

> It is this type of spirit and this type of love that can transform opposers into friends. It is this type of understanding goodwill that will transform the deep gloom of the old age into the exuberant gladness of the new age. It is this love which will bring about miracles in the hearts of men.

But before we can ever get anywhere in proximity to King's beloved community, we must first acknowledge the elephant in our midst.

King's version of the Ninety-Five Theses, his own Wittenberg moment, took place in Birmingham, Alabama, a place described by King as "the most thoroughly segregated city in the United States." A city where not only were the libraries segregated but books containing pictures of black rabbits and white rabbits together on the same page were banned from the bookshelves. It was a city, according to one famous report, where "every medium of mutual interest, every reasoned approach, every inch of middle ground" had been "fragmented by the emotional dynamite of racism." A city where bullets, bombs and burning crosses served as constant deterrents to blacks who aspired to anything greater than their assigned station of disparity. A city where vigilante mobs in white hoods collaborated with the police to reinforce the social status quo. There, five decades ago, King and his movement of nonviolent protesters staged a campaign that would rock America. Upon his arrival in the city, King was promptly arrested. But from behind bars in the city jail he composed what would become his most famous written work.

Though addressed to "My Dear Fellow Clergymen" as a cordial response to eight white religious leaders in Birmingham who criticized his presence in the city, King's "Letter from Birmingham Jail" was far more than that. King appeared to be writing not only out of the disappointment he felt upon reading the clergymen's open letter but also out of a greater concern for justice and truth. As one biographer noted, King's "Letter from Birmingham Jail" represented his "comprehensive reply at last to all the accumulated cautionings and skepticisms" that had been aimed at him from the national media, the Negro elite, Billy Graham and even the president of the United States. As such, the writing of "Letter from Birmingham Jail" was both a prophetic and cathartic undertaking. The eight white "moderate" clergymen, who favored a gradual approach to racial integration, were simply King's entryway to a broader discourse.

What becomes apparent to any serious reader of the letter is that this is not just "I Have a Dream" from an Alabama jail cell. Though King's vision of racial integration and unity is clearly present, on this occasion the Baptist preacher is more concerned about issues of discipleship and righteousness. What does it mean to live out the Christian gospel in the context of a broken, unjust society? When does the silence of people of faith become as damaging as the shouts of haters? Speaking to the eight clergymen, King offered this stark caution: "If today's church does not recapture the sacrificial spirit of the early church, it will lose its authenticity . . . and be dismissed as an irrelevant social club." It's a warning that resonates just as much now as it did then, and Christians from a variety of backgrounds continue to see the letter's urgency for the myriad challenges confronting the church in society.

"Dr. King wanted all Christians to embrace the meaning of the civil rights struggle," says Alvin Sanders, an African American who is the executive director of reconciliation in the Evangelical Free Church of America. "In the 'Letter from Birmingham Jail' he put the African American struggle squarely as part of the process of authentic discipleship. He believed the fight for justice was an essential mark of the gospel."

Julie J. Park, a University of Maryland education professor who studies race, class and religion among Asian Americans, returns to "Letter from Birmingham Jail" whenever she senses her faith needs a jolt. "King's letter reads like a kick in the stomach to me," she says. "Our churches are full of 'white moderates' like the ones who criticized King—myself included, even as a person of color. We're often too content with too small of a vision, too small of a God." She adds: "When we are too content with the status quo, we have forgotten King's vision."

KING IN COLOR

This is a book about Birmingham, Martin Luther King Jr., and the church. It is both a history and an extended reflection on a pivotal passage in the American story. In the pages that follow we'll revisit the remarkable events of 1963, listen again to Dr. King's prophetic challenge and reconsider the meaning of his legacy for the church and society. In addition to the voices of King and other key civil rights revolutionaries such as the late Fred Shuttlesworth, we'll hear from contemporary people of faith about the lingering challenges of racial reconciliation in Birmingham and beyond, and explore how the events of fifty years ago inform our lives today.

Though popular history has given us romanticized images of King bravely marching the streets of Birmingham or solemnly gazing out from his jail cell, the King we meet in Birmingham is a far more complicated figure than any photograph can convey. Sure, he's the eloquent civil rights leader who is at the height of his intellectual and elocutionary powers. But he's also a leader damaged by recent failures, burdened by the swelling weight of responsibility and not entirely certain of what his next move should be.

So many of our memories of King and the civil rights movement feature the man in crisp, black-and-white footage or photographs. "I Have a Dream," his greatest moment on video, presents that young, thrilling, black-and-white King. However, there is also film and video footage of King "in color"—during the Selma march in 1965, in the chaos of the Chicago campaign in 1966, speaking out against Vietnam in 1967, the "Mountaintop" speech on the night before his death in 1968. These polychromatic moments reveal a weary, less optimistic King. More melancholic, frustrated, burdened. This was a physically heavier King as well.

King in color represents a fuller version of the man. Birmingham foreshadows that more complex King. In fact, one of the conceits of this book is that in King's "Letter from Birmingham Jail" we can see the maturation of everything that came before and the portent of everything that would follow in the preacher's brief but remarkable thirty-nine years.

Just like Luther's memo nailed to the Wittenberg Church door, King's jailhouse epistle is a document teeming with deep and challenging ideas about theology, justice and freedom. If we allow it, we'll find that King's freestyle meditation will take us on a sweeping journey from the Birmingham, Bible Belt, Deep South of 1963 to the postracial, post-Christian, Red State-Blue State cacophony of twentieth-first-century America and beyond, with cameo appearances by everyone from Socrates, St. Augustine and St. Thomas Aquinas to Frederick Douglass, T. S. Eliot and Reinhold Niebuhr.

Birmingham stands as a monumental moment in time, capturing King at his most courageous—and most human. In his letter we can observe all the religious, philosophical and political ideas and principles that shaped his Christian vision. They are ideas and principles that we'd do well to reclaim today.

Birmingham Begins

Martin Luther King Jr.

From 1910 to 1970, more than six million African Americans left the South to settle in the northern and western regions of the United States. They left to escape the South's stubborn habits of white supremacy. They left for the promise of gainful employment in bustling cities such as Chicago and Detroit. They left because their spirits hungered for freedom. Now known as "the Great Migration," this massive exodus fundamentally transformed the cultural, economic and political demographics of the nation.

Journalists Nicholas Lemann and Isabel Wilkerson have brilliantly documented the phenomenon in their respective books *The Promised Land* and *The Warmth of Other Suns*, with Wilkerson astutely calling it an "unrecognized immigration" within our own borders. If slavery brought black people to this land against their wills and Jim Crow kept them mindful of their subservience, the Great Migration represented a mighty shaking of the South's dust from their feet. "Some came straight from the field with their King James Bibles and old twelve-string guitars," writes Wilkerson. "Still others were townspeople looking to be their fuller selves, tradesmen following their customers, pastors trailing their flocks." This was their chance to reboot the failed promises of Reconstruction and grab hold of a fresh beginning. So by train, bus and car they pointed their futures northward. Of course, the prospect of racial progress in those supposedly liberated destinations ultimately would bring new and in some ways more impenetrable obstacles than those faced in Dixie, but more on that later.

MIGRANT MEMORIES

If one thinks of the Great Migration as an immigration event, like Wilkerson describes it, then in a manner of speaking I am the son of immigrants. My late parents, who adopted me as a tot in the early 1970s, were children of the segregated South. Growing up, I sometimes felt shame at being the young son of older parents; today I recognize their advanced age as a wonderful gift, one that often provided me with firsthand lessons in black history from two original sources. My mother, a native of New Orleans, journeyed to Chicago and then Rockford, Illinois, in 1929 at the age of twenty-one. My father, who was eight years younger, hailed from Huntsville, Alabama, and found his way to Rockford in 1955. Stella Pratt and Ed Gilbreath met and married in 1956.

Along with the customary stories of how they walked great distances to school, I was also regaled with my parents' strangely wistful remembrances of segregated life in the South. Somehow the separate water fountains and backdoor entryways were never enough to drown out their sweet memories of Mama's cornbread, Papa's dreaded whippings or lazy afternoons spent fishing at the creek with bamboo poles. Still, despite the nostalgic moments, their recounting of how they trembled in the presence of some white people or avoided walking alone in certain parts of town left no question in my mind that life for a Southern black person in the Jim Crow era was much closer to hell than heaven.

Hearing my parents' stories, I always got the impression that it was better to be *from* the South than in it. Millions of black citizens apparently had the same idea. And places such as Birmingham, Alabama, no doubt helped fuel the impulse that they should pack up their bags and bolt.

BLACK MAGIC BLUES

Ironically, once upon a time Birmingham was seen as the Promised Land for poor African Americans working in south Alabama's cruel system of sharecropping, which had replaced slavery as the South's primary means of low-cost labor. Migrating north, black share-cropping families sought greater economic opportunity in central Alabama's burgeoning metropolis. Established in 1871, six years after the Civil War, Birmingham was created to be an industrial center of the New South, with steel mills and metal foundries at the heart of its economy. It was selected as the Jefferson County seat in 1873, and soon was nicknamed the "Magic City" because of its amazingly rapid growth. Along with Atlanta to the east, it became one of the two major railroad hubs of the Deep South.

Race, as has been the case in American politics from the start, played a prominent role in the city's early success. Conceived as a town where cheap, nonunionized and mostly African American labor from rural Alabama could be utilized in the city's factories, Birmingham's very foundation was built on a racial caste system designed to ensure lasting power and prosperity for its white male politicians and industrialists (who were popularly known as the "Big Mules").

When newly elected Republican president Warren G. Harding took office in 1921, he raised eyebrows when he decided to make one of his first presidential trips a visit to Birmingham to deliver a speech on race. To a crowd of more than twenty-five thousand people—with a chainlink fence separating the whites from the blacks—Harding said, "Let the black man vote if he is fit" and voiced support for anti-lynching bills pending in Congress. He added that

America would never fulfill its full potential until blacks and whites received equal treatment under the law. The Negroes applauded and cheered. The white Birminghamians offered icy silence.

By virtue of its size and origins, Birmingham would become the South's largest segregated city. Over the years, it earned another nickname too: "Bombingham," a reference to the high incidence of racially motivated bombings aimed at intimidating black citizens who forgot their place. The Smithfield community, a neighborhood on the west side of the city that became the home to many professional blacks, was attacked so often that local residents began calling it "Dynamite Hill." Birmingham's Ku Klux Klan had numerous allies embedded in the police department, and its Klan was widely considered among the most violent chapters in the South. City officials continually refused to obey the Supreme Court's landmark 1954 desegregation ruling, and political leaders across the South remarked that "blood would flow in the streets first."

The city's legendary public safety commissioner and police head Eugene "Bull" Connor was a former radio announcer and Ku Klux Klan member who entered politics in the early 1930s. He became Birmingham's commissioner in 1937 and spent more than a quarter of a century ruling the city. Connor, who earned his nickname because of his loud, bellowing voice, bragged that he knew how to keep "niggers" in their place, and most Negroes were indeed afraid to speak out against the robust Jim Crow system that defined the city. In fact, many sympathetic or "moderate" whites were afraid to speak out as well, lest they be marked as "integrationist" (a dirty word if there ever was one) or worse. Speaking out could threaten a white person's well-being—socially, economically and even mortally. But at least they could conceal their sympathies when necessary. Birmingham's Negroes, however, would always be black.

Michael W. Wesley, currently the pastor of Birmingham's Greater Shiloh Baptist Church, recalls his childhood growing up in the 1950s and 1960s in the Titusville neighborhood just south of downtown Birmingham. "It was a turbulent period of time," he says. "People remained sequestered in their own communities for fear of the circumstances that existed, and our parents constantly warned us to stay in our neighborhoods so that nothing tragic would happen."

Fresh in their minds, no doubt, was the tragedy that became symbolic of the dangers facing African Americans of all ages—the brutal murder of fourteen-year-old Emmett Till. A Chicago resident, Till was visiting relatives in rural Mississippi during the summer of 1955 when he allegedly whistled at a white woman. Days later the woman's enraged husband and his brother kidnapped the teen, beat him to a pulp, gouged out one of his eyes and finally shot him in the head. Till's body was dumped in the Tallahatchie River. The killers were later tried for murder but acquitted by an all-white jury. Till's death became an early catalyst for the nascent civil rights movement—but also an ugly reminder to African Americans of the kind of fate that could befall them if they crossed the wrong white people.

A CITY OF CHURCHES

In addition to being an industrial mecca, from its earliest days Birmingham was also a community of churches, with denominations of all stripes establishing a presence in the city and its surrounding areas. The church was especially central to the life and survival of the black community. "Churches helped black migrants adjust and accommodate to the strange new life of the city," says historian Wilson Fallin Jr., who serves as president of the Birmingham-Easonian Baptist Bible College. "As a spiritual institution, the church was the place where African Americans could go and escape the hostility of the white world in Birmingham." Indeed, it also was the one space where African Americans could experience a sense of purpose and self-worth that was missing from their daily occupations. In the church they could be leaders—deacons, trustees, ushers, choir members. In this environment, observes Fallin, they also were able to "express their deepest thoughts and highest hopes."

The church's role as a multifaceted provider of spiritual and social needs would prove even more crucial during the lean years of the Great Depression in the 1930s, when religious institutions were called on to feed, house and clothe needy individuals and families. Though pastors were naturally viewed as spiritual caretakers, by virtue of the black church's wide-ranging function in the community many of its pastors also assumed roles as strategic leaders in broader public life. Pastors, in fact, were instrumental in launching Birmingham's first black-owned banks and insurance companies. "Using their churches as a base, they established institutions to fill the economic, educational, and welfare needs of African Americans in the city," says Fallin, noting that pastors also used their churches to host mass meetings for black activist organizations.

One such organization was the National Association for the Advancement of Colored People (NAACP), which was founded in 1909 by an interracial group of civil rights leaders that included scholar W. E. B. Du Bois and journalist Ida B. Wells. The NAACP used education, journalism and the judicial system to battle racial inequality in society. It was the NAACP, for instance, that spearheaded the various lawsuits that constituted *Brown v. Board of Education* in 1954. (Thurgood Marshall, the NAACP's chief counsel, who successfully argued the case before the U.S. Supreme Court, would later become a Supreme Court Justice himself.) However, the *Brown* case—a widely felt blow against segregation and arguably the group's greatest victory—would also lead to the NAACP's temporary expulsion from Alabama, where in 1956 paranoid lawmakers banned it from operating in their state for a number of years. But as Birmingham-born journalist Diane McWhorter later observed, the

the neutralizing of Alabama's NAACP might well have been the best thing to happen to the black civil rights movement.

WILD MAN FROM BIRMINGHAM

The Rev. Fred L. Shuttlesworth, the wiry and fiery pastor of Birmingham's Bethel Baptist Church, took the state's ban of the NAACP as a personal affront. Having been raised amid the bruising poverty of Alabama's black working class, he possessed a deep-seated animosity toward racial segregation and the white-supremacist attitudes that kept it alive. "I confess to being a great criminal when it comes down to trying to get rid of segregation," he once said. "I am a notorious outlaw. I have absolutely no empathy in my heart for segregation."

Born March 18, 1922, to unmarried parents, Freddie Lee Robinson was later adopted by his stepfather, William Shuttlesworth. Fred was raised under the strict hand of his mother, Alberta, in the African Methodist Episcopal tradition. His mother, he later recalled, never allowed her nine children the luxury of sleeping in on Sunday mornings. Fred, however, was far from being a passive churchgoer. He listened intently and took to heart the sermons he heard each week. A smart and hardworking student, he graduated from Birmingham's Rosedale High School at the top of his class and went on to receive training and degrees from a variety of all-black institutions, including Cedar Grove Bible Academy in Mobile, Selma University, and Alabama State University in Montgomery. He later praised his many teachers for their vital influence on his development. "I believed in them, and they believed in me," he said. "These were the people from whom I learned to analyze things." While working as a handyman at a Birmingham medical office, he met Tuskegee Institute nursing student Ruby Keeler, whom he married in 1941.

While working variously as a truck driver and substitute teacher to support Ruby and their four children, Fred earned a preaching license and began to fill in for pastors at various Baptist churches around Alabama before taking on a permanent role at First Baptist Church in Selma in 1950. But Shuttleworth's blunt, authoritarian tone clashed with the church's deacons, and he resigned from that post after two years.

Shuttlesworth distinguished himself as an in-your-face "country preacher" with a dynamic "whoop" style of delivery. His sermons typically dealt in absolutes, emphasizing the futility of static devotion and the importance of adding action to one's faith. This got him into trouble with some of the more staid, middle-class congregations where he ministered. But working-class churchgoers loved his charisma and combative personality. In 1953 he accepted the full-time pastorate at Birmingham's Bethel Baptist Church, where he kept the pews full on a weekly basis.

An emotional leader in and out of the pulpit, Shuttlesworth soon earned a reputation as his city's most outspoken civil rights warrior. He regularly urged his parishioners to register to vote, and took it as an offense if they didn't cast their ballots. He participated in a failed effort to compel the Birmingham Police Department to hire black officers and escorted civil rights attorney Arthur Shores and college student Autherine Lucy in their ill-fated attempt to integrate the University of Alabama in Tuscaloosa. Shores's work as Birmingham's most prominent Negro lawyer led to multiple bombings of his home. Though Shores had won a 1955 case before the U.S. Supreme Court that gave Lucy the right to enter the all-white school, mob violence made it impossible for the young woman to attend. But Shuttlesworth soldiered on unfazed after each apparent setback, prodding the movement's members to keep marching forward. As the membership chairman of the Birmingham chapter of the NAACP, Shuttlesworth took the state's shuttering of the organization as an opportunity to rally local church leaders and their congregants to take action. He envisioned taking on the white establishment in a new way that combined aggressive spiritual leadership with nonviolent protest. On a warm June night in 1956, Shuttlesworth led a mass meeting of more than a thousand people at Sardis Missionary Baptist Church, where he said white leaders could ban the NAACP but they could not ban "the determination in people's minds and hearts to be free." By the end of the meeting a new organization had been born—the Alabama Christian Movement for Human Rights (ACMHR). The movement's seven-point "Declaration of Principles" expressed their "determination to press forward persistently for Freedom and Democracy" and made it clear that their mission was not to "become enemies of the White People" but to "seek Guidance from our Heavenly Father" and to pursue "from all men, Goodwill and understanding." The white media, which had caught wind of the mass meeting, viewed the ACMHR's formation as a brazen flouting of the NAACP ruling—and they were correct.

As president of the fledgling ACMHR, Shuttlesworth set out to make an immediate statement, despite warnings from attorney Arthur Shores and others that the group's actions could open them to arrest. Shuttlesworth welcomed it: "Somebody has to go to jail," he said. Emboldened by the nonviolent bus boycott in Montgomery that had made national headlines, Shuttlesworth decided the group should press for the desegregation of Birmingham's buses. Shuttlesworth and fifty other ACMHR members were arrested that December as they attempted to "ride integrated" on the city buses (one of many arrests to follow for Shuttlesworth). City officials pushed back with intensity against the ACMHR's campaign, keeping the effort tied up in the courts. But a precedent had been set in Montgomery. It would not be until December 1959 that the federal courts ruled in favor of the ACMHR, but it was a victory for Shuttlesworth nonetheless. His persistence served noticed to white Birmingham that the civil rights movement was alive and well in the city.

For his efforts Shuttlesworth became a prime target of Bull Connor and the Ku Klux Klan. On Christmas night 1956 an enormous dynamite blast went off in the space between Bethel Baptist and the church parsonage. With Shuttlesworth and his family inside, the parsonage roof collapsed and the house was essentially destroyed. Miraculously, the Shuttlesworths escaped with only minor injuries. Later a white police officer on the scene (whom Shuttlesworth suspected was also a member of the Klan) told him, "Reverend, if I was you, I'd get out of town as quick as I could." But the assault only bolstered the preacher's resolve. "If God could save me through this," he told the officer, "then I'm gonna stay here and clear this up. I wasn't saved to run." The Bethel congregation rebuilt the parsonage but added a sentry box on the front porch where men from the church volunteered to stand watch every night. At least one other bombing attempt followed, but Shuttlesworth escaped harm again when a fast-thinking watchman moved the dynamite to the middle of the street and ran.

In 1957 Fred and Ruby Shuttlesworth were the first black parents in Birmingham to try to enroll their children in a white school. Before they could get to the entrance of Phillips High School, a horde of Klansmen descended on the family and trounced Fred with chains and brass knuckles. Ruby was stabbed in the hip. Meanwhile, the Birmingham police were nowhere to be found. Fred was beaten into half-consciousness and later said he could not remember his friends dragging him back to his car to save his life.

Moments like these only added to the Shuttlesworth legend. As his biographer Andrew Manis noted, "In keeping with the biblical theme of deliverance, Shuttlesworth was a Daniel in his own right. He repeatedly put himself in the lion's den, often saying matter-of-factly, 'I tried to get killed in Birmingham.'" Fred Shuttlesworth understood that only a leader who was not afraid to die could effectively battle the massive forces of racism that oppressed blacks in Birmingham. This courageous abandon would later earn him the nickname "the Wild Man from Birmingham."

LIKE GETTING RELIGION

The *Brown v. Board of Education* decision in 1954 swept through the South like an idea whose time had finally come. In Fred Shuttlesworth's words, it was "like getting religion again." People who had once felt the hope squeezed out of them suddenly had a renewed faith—a faith "that we could be accepted into the mainstream."

This fresh optimism went a long way in terms of jumpstarting indigenous movements for change. And like geek communities on the Internet, these sundry localized efforts often inspired and sustained each other in a mutualistic fashion. More than fifty years before Facebook or Twitter, these local movements received their sustaining connection through the intricate network of African American pastors who nurtured relationships at annual denominational conventions and often traveled to other cities to "guest preach" at their friends' churches. Alabama featured an especially rich collection of prominent congregations, with its plethora of churches in Birmingham, Huntsville, Mobile and Montgomery, among other metro areas. To Shuttlesworth's way of thinking, the civil rights movement's jurisdiction was without borders. Accordingly, he sought collaboration with other local efforts whenever possible. And, of course, the one that captured everyone's attention in 1955 was taking place just ninety miles south of Birmingham in Montgomery.

Shuttlesworth had been present at Montgomery's Holt Street Baptist Church on the evening of December 5, 1955, when the Montgomery Improvement Association (MIA) was created to initiate the bus boycott. He was among the lineup of preachers to briefly address the enormous crowd that spilled out of the sanctuary onto the street. At Alabama State College, Shuttlesworth had

been classmates with Ralph Abernathy, the young pastor of First
Baptist of Montgomery, who helped organize the mass meeting.
That connection had helped bring him to town. But it was the
young preacher from Atlanta who wowed everyone that evening,
especially Shuttlesworth. "It was like an electrifying revival," he
said. "Several people spoke, but when Dr. King got up there
speaking about nonviolence in his beautiful rhetoric . . . it was to
become the language of the movement."

With that, Shuttlesworth was sold. He mobilized Birmingham's
black churches to provide financial assistance to the MIA campaign
and began traveling to Montgomery weekly to huddle with Abernathy and King. He took note of King's strategy and eagerly sought
to adapt it for his own purposes in Birmingham. Though the two
men would never become close friends and at moments uncomfortable tension would creep into their interactions, they nonetheless came to respect each other as dynamic leaders of the cause.
For Shuttlesworth, part of that respect was a grudging recognition
that what King was doing could be bigger than Montgomery—
heck, bigger than Alabama. He would continue waging his own
local battles against segregation in Birmingham, but he saw in King
the future of the war. "In Montgomery, I think all the elements
came together," Shuttlesworth later remarked. "There was the idea,
there was the man, then there was God's power." When those three
things converge, he said, "then it's time for a movement."

The Making of Martin

Martin Luther King Jr.

The two men most responsible for the Birmingham revolution could not have been more different. Fred Shuttlesworth had been born to a single mother in the stifling poverty of rural Alabama; Martin Luther King Jr. was born into a two-parent home in the polished African American environs of Atlanta, Georgia. Shuttlesworth worked an assortment of blue-collar jobs while attending all-black colleges across Alabama; King graduated from Atlanta's prestigious Morehouse College before going on to a predominantly white seminary and postgraduate school in the Northeast. Shuttlesworth was a Methodist-turned-Baptist who toiled as an itinerant preacher at congregations around Alabama before finding a stable pulpit in Birmingham; King was the son, grandson and great-grandson of Baptist preachers whose pedigree and PhD gave him his choice of attractive preaching jobs at middle-class congregations in both the North and South.

But perhaps the most striking difference between the two men was in the tendencies of their personalities: Shuttlesworth was a hell-raiser, an in-your-face firebrand who had little patience for talk that wasn't accompanied by determined action; King was a diplomat, a cautious pragmatist who sought to thoroughly analyze

a situation before acting. A mutual friend summed up their con-
trasting approaches this way: "Martin knew how to say it; Fred
know how to do it." The extent to which these dissimilar leaders
were able to borrow and learn from one another speaks directly to
the effectiveness of the Birmingham movement.

Their respective hometowns also offered hints about their
styles: Birmingham, the post–Civil War city founded as a center
of industrial scrappiness; Atlanta, the crown jewel of Dixie that
had survived the ravages of the war and went on to reinvent
itself as a city incorporating the best of the Old and New Souths.
In my attempt to understand Martin Luther King Jr.'s fateful assignment in Birmingham, I traveled to both cities. But I started
where King started—in Atlanta's "Sweet Auburn" district. King's
childhood home, now a popular tourist destination, is surrounded by other residences of varying size and repair. A string
of renovated "shotgun" style row houses, located on the other
side of Auburn Avenue, seem frozen in the gentle charm of King's
boyhood days. Standing on the twenty-first-century version of
the street, I strained to imagine the *real* King—*real* meaning the
boy who played ball with his friends, practiced piano in the
family room and received epic spankings from his father when
he misbehaved.

The Scottish writer Thomas Carlyle famously said, "The history
of the world is but the biography of great men." If this is so, King's
origins probably hold useful clues not only about his development
as a leader but also about the starts and stops of our nation when it
comes to matters of race and justice. There are, of course, many
excellent biographies of King and his work (I list some of them at
the end of this book), but in the interest of exploring the Birmingham story, it might be helpful here to briefly note some of the
key themes and experiences that defined King's childhood, education and early life. Here are fourteen that stand out.

1. Before he was Martin, he was Michael. He was born "Michael Luther King Jr." on January 15, 1929, in Atlanta, Georgia, the middle child of the Reverend Michael Luther King Sr. and Alberta Williams King. In 1934 Rev. King, the pastor of Atlanta's prestigious Ebenezer Baptist Church, was one of ten Baptist ministers who traveled first to the Holy Land and then to Germany. During the trip the senior King "discovered" the Protestant Reformer Martin Luther and was immediately captivated by the German priest's faith and grit. Upon returning to the States, he gradually changed both his name and his five-year-old son's to Martin Luther King, in what can only be described as a gutsy statement about his perception of himself and his expectations for his young namesake. The man who would become affectionately (and fearsomely) known as "Daddy King" clearly had a dream for himself and his son.

2. He came from a lineage of social-minded preachers. Daddy King's father-in-law, Rev. Adam Daniel (A. D.) Williams, had pastored Ebenezer Baptist from 1894 until his death in 1931, growing the church from thirteen congregants to more than four hundred by 1903. The son of a slave preacher, Williams was a trailblazer in advocating "a distinctive African American version of the social gospel"—that is, the application of the Christian gospel to the material concerns of society. According to one King scholar, Williams promoted "a strategy that combined elements of [Booker T.] Washington's emphasis on black business development and W. E. B. Du Bois's call for civil rights activism." He also prayed—and, indeed, expected—that his new grandson would someday follow in that tradition. Daddy King, having been mentored in the ministry by his father-in-law, possessed a similar concern for the Negro poor and oppressed, and he preached sermons that combined equal parts self-empowerment and social protest.

3. He was a child of privilege—relatively speaking. By most accounts the King home was warm and loving, notwithstanding

Daddy King's authoritarian presence. After "Little Mike" became Martin at five, he took on the alternate nickname M. L. As a middle child, he grew up in between his older sister, Christine, who was sixteen months his senior, and his younger brother, Alfred Daniel (A. D.), who arrived seventeen months after him. The family lived in a modest two-story house (that Alberta Williams King inherited from her parents) located in Sweet Auburn, a middle-class African American neighborhood that was home to some of Atlanta's most prominent black leaders in business, education and the church. King described his upbringing as somewhat privileged: "Not wealthy really, but Negro-wealthy."

4. *He discovered the pain of racism at an early age.* Daddy King became a towering figure in black Atlanta, a man unafraid of the white racism that sporadically infringed on the sanctity of community life in Sweet Auburn. Martin would never forget the moments of fearless and principled protest that he observed in his father. Once, when Daddy King was pulled over by an insolent traffic cop who addressed him as "boy," Daddy King motioned toward young Martin sitting beside him and declared unflinchingly, "That's a boy. I'm a man." Even more impactful were the moments when racism touched young Martin directly, without the buffer of Daddy King. Preserved in his adult memory were flashbacks of the white friend with whom he had played since the age of three. One day, when they were six, the boy informed Martin that they couldn't be friends any longer because his father had forbidden him from socializing with "Negroes." Heartbroken and confused, King shared the news with his parents over dinner. "For the first time," he remembered, "I was made aware of the existence of a race problem."

Suddenly, he began to take special notice of the swimming pools and parks and downtown movie theaters that were off limits to Negroes. When Martin was eight, a white woman at a downtown department store suddenly turned and slapped him. "You are that little nigger that stepped on my foot," she snapped, apparently mistaking Martin for some other Negro child whom she felt entitled to strike. Martin knew not to say anything.

5. *As a youth he made a vow to hate all white people.* Brooding and introspective, the young King struggled to make sense of a world that told him he was a dignified *somebody* on the one hand but an inconsequential *nobody* on the other. "My parents would always tell me that I should not hate the white man, but that it was my duty as a Christian to love him," King later recalled. But he wondered: "How could I love a race of people who hated me?" Consequently, King resolved to return their hate in kind. "I was determined to hate every white person," he said. And those feelings continued to swell throughout his youth.

6. *He was turned off by black preaching.* Raised under the religious pieties of the black Baptist tradition, King came out of what was basically a fundamentalist, evangelical church, as was the case for most Protestant congregations in the black Southern tradition during King's formative years. In the words of theologian H. Malcolm Newton, "They taught the Bible at Ebenezer Baptist Church. That was [King's] roots." Still, by his teen years he had developed a supercilious distaste for his father's church and the black preaching tradition. He harbored contempt for the Southern Negro preacher's hysterical "whooping," the wild emotionalism and the low level of intellectual training.

7. *He entered college at the age of fifteen and became an agnostic.* A precocious pupil, Martin skipped two grades and by fifteen had passed the entrance exam to the historically black Morehouse College. Even though he was at the school where his father, grandfather and great-grandfather had gone before him, he arrived on the all-male campus eager to escape the burden of his family profession. Though both his grandfather and father had de-

termined early on that he would follow in their footsteps, King entered Morehouse as a self-proclaimed agnostic, with intentions of pursuing a medical degree before switching to sociology, hoping to later parlay it into a career in law.

8. As a college student, he loved a good party. Though only an average student at Morehouse, he established himself as a smooth speaker and an even smoother dresser. At just under five feet, seven inches, King was relatively short in physical stature. Yet his charm and impeccable grooming evoked a physical confidence that went beyond height. A few years later, for example, upon first meeting King, Coretta Scott, his future wife (then a student at the New England Conservatory of Music), famously recalled her initial surprise at his appearance: "He was so young looking and short," she said. "But as he talked, he just grew taller and taller." At Morehouse, however, King used his way with words for less-honorable purposes. He earned a reputation as a ladies' man and a guy who loved a good party. For a while King and several of his friends began an informal playboy club which they called "the Wreckers" because, as King wryly told someone at the time, "We wreck girls." When I first discovered this tidbit, I had to stop and think. One could only imagine the sophistication of the mack M. L. employed to win the affections of bewitched young women from nearby Spelman College.

9. Interracial student experiences changed his view of white people. But King had his missional side as well, and this is what eventually won out. He participated in integrated student groups that were concerned with equal rights for all Americans. This was significant because not only did it address a topic that had concerned him since childhood but it represented his growth beyond that disillusioned promise he had made to himself earlier "to hate every white person." He later recalled, "The wholesome relations we had in the Intercollegiate Council convinced me that we had many white persons as allies, particularly among the younger generation." He added, "I had been ready to resent the whole white race, but as I got to see more of white people, my resentment softened, and a spirit of cooperation took its place."

10. Key African American mentors helped shape his destiny. King forged special bonds with two African American leaders at Morehouse—the college president, Dr. Benjamin Mays, a nationally renowned theological scholar, and religion and philosophy professor Dr. George Kelsey. Both men challenged King to stop and think, he said. "Both were ministers, both deeply religious, and yet both were learned men, aware of all the trends of modern thinking. I could see in their lives the ideal of what I wanted a minister to be." Through their influence, King read the nineteenth-century American poet and philosopher Henry David Thoreau's 1849 essay "On Civil Disobedience" for the first time and was transfixed by his assertion that individuals should not allow governments to weaken their consciences or compel them to become unwitting agents of injustice. Thoreau was driven, to some degree, by his disgust with slavery and the Mexican-American War. King said he was so intrigued by the concept of refusing cooperation with an immoral system that he reread the book multiple times. Later, as a student at Crozer Theological Seminary, King heard a sermon by Howard University president Dr. Mordecai Johnson that also revolutionized his thinking. Johnson, who had just returned from a trip to India, spoke passionately about the life and teachings of the Indian civil rights leader Mohandas Gandhi, who applied nonviolent direct action to liberate his people from British imperialism. Johnson's message about Gandhi and India was so dynamic, said King, "that I left the meeting and bought a half-dozen books on Gandhi's life and works." It's interesting to note that two of King's most significant nonblack influences were introduced to him through the teaching and preaching of black Christian intellectuals.

11. He could not escape the influence of his Christian upbringing.
During the summer of 1947, before his last year at Morehouse,
King made official the call that had been stirring within him all
along—he would enter the Christian ministry. It was not an emotional, Damascus Road–type decision. Rather, for King it was a ra-
tional conclusion that the church was still the most effective way to
serve humanity and change society. He would later remark that
"the effects of the noble moral and ethical ideals" that he was raised
under "were real and precious" to him, and that "even in moments
of theological doubt" he could not turn away from them.

*12. His "liberal" education in the North fueled his activism in
the South.* King's northern sojourn, from 1948 to 1954, took him
out of the South for the first extended period in his life. His education at Crozer Theological Seminary and Boston University took
him deeper into the study of liberal theology. This time would
prove vital to his formation as a both a Christian thinker and
social activist. He entered Crozer, for instance, as part of what he
described as "a serious intellectual quest for a method to eliminate
social evil." At Crozer, King engaged in an intensive personal
study of the social and ethical theories of Plato, Aristotle, St. Augustine, St. Thomas Aquinas, Rousseau, Hobbes, Bentham, Mill
and Locke—many of whom would later find their way into King's
famous Birmingham letter. As a PhD student in systematic theology at Boston University, King immersed himself even more ex-
plicitly in philosophical and religious schools of thought that both
supported and challenged his basic ideas about God, humanity
and justice. The recurring criticism leveled against King by conservative Christians that he subscribed to a social gospel or that
his theology was too liberal perhaps ignores the value of that
suspect theology to the development of King's message and methodology, which according to Duke Divinity School scholar Richard
Lischer blended the "African-Baptist tradition that formed him as

a preacher and the liberal theological tradition that shaped him as an American religious activist."

King had indeed gone to schools that proffered a host of progressive views, and this certainly had an impact on his beliefs—but as Christian writer and Atlanta native Philip Yancey has observed about Southern Christians' disparaging attitude toward King's education: "We said that Daddy King had raised Martin right, but that the liberal Crozer Seminary up north had polluted his mind. . . . We never asked ourselves what conservative seminaries might have accepted Martin's application back then." Though segregation prevented King from considering more conservative Christian schools, one wonders where the civil rights movement would have gone had King *not* encountered Edgar S. Brightman's and L. Harold DeWolf's personalist theology, Walter Rauschenbusch's Social Gospel and Reinhold Niebuhr's Christian Realism.

13. Though a brilliant student, he was a sloppy scholar. King's research as a doctoral student was far from groundbreaking or original. In fact, it's now commonly known that his dissertation and other academic writings contained glaring examples of derivative material and even plagiarism. These controversial instances of missing or incomplete citations indicated a pattern of sloppy scholarship, but the very sort of content that King borrowed (writings by his own professors or popular pieces that he knew they would be familiar with) suggests that he was in no way attempting to pull the wool over anyone's eyes. Rather, King's missteps, while troublesome, point to an overreliance on the oral tradition from which he hailed as a preacher—a tradition that regularly appropriated and remixed multiple sources to create a dynamic exegetical narrative. Could it be that the grad student was more interested in gathering intellectual ammo for his theological arsenal than doing the tedious busywork of a scholar? Possibly, but it's still evident according to Lischer that despite his "carelessness

and lapses in academic honesty, King's immersion in academic theology was real and significant for his development as a preacher."
Failures in academic protocol notwithstanding, his absorption of a
wide range of texts helped him articulate an original vision and
"provided the vocabulary and conceptual framework of his sermons
. . . and his larger message to the nation."

14. *A sense of duty led him to resist the temptation to stay in the*
North. After a brief dalliance with the notion of pursuing a career
as a professor, King decided that he would follow through with his
plans to become a Baptist pastor. As his studies in Boston wound
down, he also came to the conclusion that he and his new wife
Coretta had "a moral obligation" to return to the South to help
solve the nation's grievous race problem. Coretta, on the other
hand, preferred staying in the North, where she felt there would be
more opportunities to realize her dream of becoming a professional
singer. A native of Alabama, she dreaded the idea of returning to
the dispiriting segregation of the Deep South. The thought of
someday raising children there especially bothered her. Though
King left open the possibility of pastoring in a northern city, in
truth his desire was to return to the South. And after days of vigorous debate and prayer, he prevailed. "[We] agreed that, in spite
of the disadvantages and inevitable sacrifices, our greatest service
could be rendered in our native South," King said.

GOING TO ALABAMA

These fourteen points by no means capture the totality of King's
early years, but in different ways they shed light on the heart and
mind of the young man who would later emerge in Alabama as a
transformational figure. As he completed his PhD at Boston University, King explored leads at churches in Tennessee and Alabama.
One appealing prospect, Dexter Avenue Baptist, a prominent
middle-class congregation in Montgomery, invited the young doc-

toral candidate down to preach for the parishioners. King decided to share with them "The Three Dimensions of a Complete Life," which was his favorite sermon at the time. "Life at its best is a great triangle," King declared to the Dexter worshipers. "At one angle stands the individual person, at the other angle stands other persons, and at the tip top stands God. Unless these three are concatenated, working harmoniously together in a single life, that life is incomplete."

Dexter's worshipers—and, more importantly, its deacons—were impressed by the young preacher's superb homiletic abilities, as well as his humble demeanor. King liked them too. Though the congregation was slightly stiff in comparison to Ebenezer Baptist in Atlanta, he fancied the idea of leading such an influential congregation in a major Southern city. Coretta didn't like the fact that the church was only fifty miles away from her hometown, and Daddy King didn't like the fact that it *wasn't* Ebenezer. But when an offer was extended, King accepted. In September 1954 the couple moved to Montgomery.

Dexter Avenue Baptist Church would mark the official beginning of Martin Luther King Jr.'s career as a pastor. No one could begin to imagine the other occupation it would soon precipitate.

Montgomery Miracle

SOMETHING HAPPENED TO ME in Atlanta that helped me better imagine what people like Martin Luther King Jr., Fred Shuttlesworth and Rosa Parks must have felt throughout their lives in the South. It's absurd for me to presume that I—a black man in the twenty-first century who can sit anywhere he'd like to on a bus and go generally anyplace he chooses—could begin to feel anything akin to the indignity and oppression that confronted African Americans from their era. I know that. But this incident prompted me to wonder what they experienced as real human beings, not iconic heroes of a movement.

I've never been arrested for anything, but I have been pulled over by police for speeding and other traffic violations. My most recent violation occurred in April 2012, while I was visiting Atlanta on a research trip for this book. I had spent the day blissfully immersed in Morehouse College's MLK Collection at the Woodruff Library. As I sifted through digital files featuring a treasure-trove of original documents, many from Dr. King's own typewriter or pen, it felt like one of those days when everything was clicking. After hours of nonstop research, I gathered my things to leave. But before driving back to my hotel, I took a detour to search for a used bookstore that I had spotted online. (Confession: I love visiting used bookstores whenever I travel.) The rental car agent at the airport had given me a red Chevy compact with Texas plates, so my *out-of-town-ness* was on full display as I drove around strange sections of Atlanta. In my hunt for the store, I managed to get lost. Attempting to make my way back to I-20, I turned on my signal and prepared to make a left turn onto the connecting road. I could see the police officer in the squad car sitting across the road from me. I watched him the whole time that I waited at the traffic light. In fact, when I finally made the turn, I tried to be extra careful, just to make sure I wasn't violating any rules. When he zipped behind me and turned on his lights, I wondered what I had done. I pulled into the parking lot of what appeared to be a boarded-up liquor store (this wasn't the nicest side of Atlanta) and sat nervously for what seemed like two or three minutes. Finally, the officer got out of his squad car. I watched in my rearview mirror as the large, towering man with a blonde crew cut made his way to my car. He was imposing. He was white. And he had that kind of unsympathetic look that let me know right off this wasn't going to be my day. I learned long ago with cops only to speak when spoken to, so I smiled nervously and waited for him to talk.

"You made an illegal left turn back there," he said. "I'm sorry, sir," I said with a sudden obsequiousness that surprised even me. "I'm visiting from Chicago, and I got a bit lost. I honestly did not see the sign." He offered no compassion. Instead, he walked to his car and returned five minutes later with a $200 citation. I knew my insurance company would be delighted. But what was worse was the vibe I received from the officer; you would've thought I had a record of serial offenses. When I handed him my driver's license, he looked at it and scowled, "This license is expired," as if it confirmed his suspicions about me. I asked him to turn it over, where he could see the official Illinois sticker that extended the expiration date. He only offered an annoyed grunt in reply.

By the end of my interaction with the officer, I felt awful. It didn't help that I had spent the day reading about Dr. King's encounters with the law and the gigantic wall of enmity that existed between the police and the African American community throughout the twentieth-century civil rights movement. I did not want race to enter my thinking that day. I had, after all, made an illegal turn—I accepted responsibility for my absent-minded mistake. But I still couldn't shake the feeling that the officer had approached me with a prearranged contempt. Did he treat everyone he pulled over that way, or was my skin color a factor? Such has been the dilemma with African Americans and the law for much of our nation's history.

The next morning I drove the 150 miles from Atlanta to Birmingham to continue my research. My nerves were on edge the entire way. *I cannot afford to get pulled over again*, I kept saying to myself. Two days later, on my way back to the Atlanta airport, I stopped at a service station to refuel my rental car and spotted an African American police officer. My journalist's curiosity kicked in and I thought to myself, *I should talk to him*. I debated with myself for a moment before finally deciding to do it. "Good afternoon, officer," I said, remembering to keep my hands out in the open where he could see them. "I know this might sound crazy, but may I ask you a question?" He said yes and patiently listened to me recount my experience with the white cop from two days earlier. "I'm from Chicago," I told him, "and I don't want to sound paranoid, but I wondered if that officer's harsh attitude had something to do with race." I asked him if there is just a blanket policy to issue a citation for a careless mistake like mine, or did the officer have any room for making a judgment call. He told me that in those types of situations, if no one was injured or it didn't cause a major disruption, it's left up to the discretion of the officer. He said he didn't know if it had anything to do with race, but he speculated that the white officer simply didn't believe me. He added, "I probably would've issued a warning and asked you to be more careful." I told him I wished he had been the policeman that pulled me over that day.

WHEN THE LAW IS AGAINST YOU

Like so many issues today in the realm of race relations, the topic of "racial profiling" is a subject fraught with emotion. Almost any black person—especially black men—can tell stories of being stopped and questioned by the police for no good reason that they could ascertain. The 2012 slaying of Florida teenager Trayvon Martin spun many parents into a state of anxiety about the safety of their black sons and daughters. Then there's profiling and the immigration issue. The sticking point of the strict immigration laws that some states (including Alabama) have been pushing is the license it may give police to target members of the Latino community who might look illegal. Do police really target some groups based on race, or are they simply targeting people who strike them as suspicious regardless of ethnicity? Are these two things sometimes one and the same?

In the Jim Crow South of twentieth-century America there was no confusion about whether racial profiling existed—it was an unequivocal fact of life for the Negro community. To be black meant being born with the law against you, no matter how law-abiding you were. It meant having no dependable recourse for justice. It meant having to strive every day to stay within the good graces of capricious authorities, who at any moment—and for no justifiable reason—might decide to deny you basic rights, throw you in jail, physically assault you, or worse. This, for me, was the most unsettling reality of the civil rights era: if you were black, the system was rigged. You had no way to win. Your best hope was to suck it up and learn how to navigate the injustices. This is what an obstinate Rosa Parks decided she was through with when she refused to surrender her seat on the bus on December 1, 1955.

At its root the great mission of the civil rights movement in America has been an issue of the law—confronting it, defying it, exposing it and squeezing it until it finally agrees to do what it's supposed to do. This was Dr. King's lesson from the Montgomery, Alabama, bus boycott—his dramatic initiation into large-scale civil rights leadership.

UPRISING IN MONTGOMERY

Looked at one way, for a twenty-five-year-old black man King had a pretty good thing going for himself. Fresh out of graduate school with his PhD in philosophy, and newly married to a beautiful woman, he was set to begin his career as a pastor at one of Montgomery's most esteemed black churches. When the young Atlanta-bred minister officially arrived on October 31, 1954, to take over the pastorate at Dexter Avenue Baptist Church, most knew he was a brilliant young scholar with superior preaching skills, but beyond the typical fanfare that accompanied the welcoming of a new pastor, it was supposed to be a rather routine appointment.

By all accounts, Dexter was a prestigious African American congregation, thoroughly middle and upper class with a reputation as a socially refined "big-shots church." But the church was also known as a "preacher killer," regularly chasing out of town pastors who rocked the boat too much or did not conform to its somewhat conservative and snooty predilections. Dexter's well-to-do Negroes knew how to coexist with the white supremacist system of Montgomery society, and for them life was generally good. So for a fresh-faced preacher to come into town and take on the leadership of not just their church but the burgeoning civil rights movement was not something they reasonably would have signed up for.

It was also unlikely that anyone would've predicted that Rosa Parks would provide the initial spark. The seamstress and local

NAACP secretary was tired when she chose to defy Montgomery's segregation laws by refusing to give up her seat on the crowded bus to a white passenger. Her act of bold resistance had consequences that would upset her community's rigid social order and reach far beyond Montgomery.

Montgomery, which had been the first capital of the Confederacy during the Civil War, was saddled with a severe Jim Crow oppression that tainted even the most basic cross-racial interaction. "The doctrine of white supremacy cast a pall over the entire city of Montgomery," writes King scholar Troy Jackson. "Although a handful spoke against the system, the vast majority of whites either wholeheartedly endorsed segregation or tacitly sanctioned its existence." The situation was grave within the African American community as well. "Montgomery's black community was divided," adds Jackson. In addition to bickering among community leaders, class divisions between Montgomery's black professionals and blue-collar workers also were in play. Taken together, these factors created a difficult environment for any sort of organized effort to challenge the city's segregationist system. Small factions of blacks had unsuccessfully attempted to challenge the white Montgomery machine in the past, demanding integrated schools after the 1954 *Brown v. the Board of Education* ruling and protesting the arrest of teenager Claudette Colvin, who preceded Parks by nine months in her refusal to give up her seat on a segregated bus. But, in general, Montgomery had remained stuck in its ways.

Until now.

With Mrs. Parks's arrest as a rallying point, an alliance of the city's Negro ministers and business leaders, including First Baptist Church pastor Ralph Abernathy and the passionate Pullman railroad porter E. D. Nixon, gathered together to develop a serious response. They called their group the Montgomery Improvement Association (MIA) and chose King as the president. He was promptly charged with addressing the Montgomery campaign's first mass meeting at Holt Street Baptist Church on December 5.

Martin and Coretta were still settling into their new life in Montgomery—setting up a home in the Dexter parsonage on South Jackson Street, making new friends in the community and adjusting to their all-consuming roles as parents to their first child, Yolanda. It was not an ideal time for Martin to lead a citywide campaign. Now twenty-six years old, he knew his speech at the meeting would be the most important "sermon" of his life up to that point. Indeed, that night more than five thousand people filled the sanctuary, overflowed into the basement and spilled out onto the surrounding property outside, where they listened to the proceedings via a makeshift PA system. Having scrambled to prepare his thoughts, King delivered a message designed to unify the black community while inspiring them to withhold their patronage from the city's public transportation system until it was completely desegregated. It was the first time most of the people in the large crowd heard him speak publicly, and they erupted in enthusiastic "amens" and applause throughout the message.

The Montgomery campaign would continue for 381 days before successfully concluding on December 20, 1956, with a federal court ruling that would lead to Montgomery's bus segregation laws being declared unconstitutional. Before it was over, King and his cohort were arrested, threatened, bombed and generally harassed. As the chief MIA spokesman, King was routinely snubbed and disrespected by the city's white officials and promised concessions that never came. It was not an easy 381 days, but the campaign prevailed due in part to King's leadership, the thousands who committed to staying off public transportation and the campaign's dedication to prayer. A year after the boycott, in 1957, when the evangelist Billy Graham invited King to lead a prayer at his Madison Square Garden crusade, he eagerly asked King how he managed to keep the boycott so peaceful. "Prayer," said King, simply. "Montgomery was a movement of prayer."

ON THE WHITE SIDE

Robert Graetz, a local Lutheran minister who befriended King during the tumultuous Montgomery campaign, remembers those days well. In 1955, when the boycott was in its embryonic stages, Graetz had a decision to make. As the white pastor of the all-black Trinity Lutheran Church, he could either remain silent and preserve his privileges as a white man in the community, or forfeit his family's peace and safety by identifying himself with his Negro parishioners. Graetz, lanky and sandy-haired, chose to remain faithful to his flock and became the only white leader publicly active in the boycott. Graetz, today in his eighties and back in Montgomery after numerous pastorates in Ohio, explained it this way: "My family and I had to get involved. If we had remained aloof, our effectiveness as spiritual leaders in the black community would have disintegrated."

His involvement with the bus boycott introduced Graetz to King. "From the first time I met him, I was impressed," Graetz told me in an interview. "In terms of his intellect, speaking skills, and ability to motivate people, he was at the top all by himself. He had the remarkable ability to inspire everyone in his presence." King also thought highly of Graetz, whom he described in his book *Stride Toward Freedom* as the "boyish-looking white minister" of a Negro congregation who was "a constant reminder" that there were white people living out the "love-thy-neighbor-as-thyself" principle of Christianity in their daily lives.

Graetz remembered that King and his wife had only been in Montgomery for a year when he was tapped to head up the boycott. According to Graetz, King was recruited partly because of his charismatic leadership skills and partly because of his newness to the community—he hadn't made any enemies yet.

As the movement picked up steam, angry segregationists cracked down on the protesters. King's home and those of other Negro leaders were bombed. Graetz was called a "nigger lover" and was frequently awakened at night by the blast of pipe bombs tossed into his yard. He said the whites of the extreme "Klan mentality" were a minority; most whites in Montgomery were simply indifferent. But those who were racist made it clear that they would do everything possible to keep Negroes in their place. There was an even smaller number of Montgomery's whites who were "neo-abolitionists"—those who did everything possible to change the plight of blacks. "They were not nearly as outspoken," said Graetz, "because as soon as people spoke up, they were fired from their jobs, or their mortgages were foreclosed. Even a rumor that a white businessman was helping black people was enough to put him out of business."

Many of Montgomery's white leaders likely shared the attitude of Joe Azbell, who was an editor with the *Montgomery Advertiser*. In a sentiment that apparently was pretty common at the time, Azbell was taken aback by the uprising in the black community. He believed the Negro protesters were ungrateful for all the good things whites had done for them over the years. This was similar, I discovered, to the way many of Birmingham's white leaders would later feel about the African Americans in their city—"Why is this awful King man poisoning the minds of our good Negroes?"

But despite the intransigence of the white community, King and his movement ultimately secured integrated busing in Montgomery through a federal lawsuit, and blacks throughout the South were buoyed by the triumph. Soon King, along with fellow Montgomery pastor Ralph Abernathy and other Negro Christian leaders, formed the Southern Christian Leadership Conference (SCLC), a national civil rights organization. "The thing that is often overlooked is that the civil rights movement was a *church* movement," said Graetz. "The leaders were pastors, and the mass meetings were church services, with prayers, hymns, sermons, and offerings."

THE CRUCIBLE OF LEADERSHIP

In the early stages of the Montgomery campaign, King struggled with uncertainty and doubt about whether he had what it took to lead such a massive and demanding campaign. The struggle became so real that at moments he considered removing himself from the situation, especially as death threats, shattered windows and burning crosses began to become a regular occurrence. He had to think about his family, which now included his infant daughter, Yolanda, who was born in November 1955. King also was concerned about Daddy King, who was now making frequent trips to Montgomery to check on his son. "Every time I saw him I went through a deep feeling of anxiety," said King, "because I knew that my every move was driving him deeper and deeper into a state of worry."

A turning point came in January 1956. As the often chaotic excitement propelling the Montgomery boycott reached its most intense levels, King received a phone call at midnight from a white man who called him a "nigger" and threatened to kill him and "blow up" his home. Unable to sleep, King paced the floor before settling in his kitchen for a cup of coffee that he was too nervous to drink. He wanted to quit. But he had no idea how to remove himself from the campaign without looking like a coward. King said he felt weak and helpless. He realized his only hope was the One who could "make a way out of no way." He needed to have a one-on-one encounter with Jesus, one that didn't come on the coattails of his mother and father's faith but that belonged to him alone. He bowed his head over the kitchen table and prayed a prayer that he said he'd always remember: "Lord, I'm down here trying to do what's right," he prayed, "but I have nothing left." The voice of Jesus came quietly, King said, but he heard it: "Martin Luther, stand up for righteousness. Stand up for justice. Stand up for truth. And lo, I will be with you. Even until the end of the world." After that "vision in the kitchen," as chroniclers came to call it, King said his doubt ceased. He was ready to confront the trials and tribulations that would await him.

According to King scholar Lewis Baldwin, this supernatural event further confirmed to King that times of struggle and uncertainty are often precisely the times when God visits us as we seek him through solitude and prayer. In that moment of quiet anguish, King found new assurance and purpose through the power of prayer, and came to understand for himself "what it meant to follow Jesus Christ as a passionate disciple."

Throughout the yearlong campaign, King also was able to test drive the ideas of nonviolent resistance and civil disobedience that he had studied and had witnessed in the activism of Gandhi, the writings of Thoreau and the New Testament teachings of Jesus. He became convinced that what they were doing in Montgomery was directly related to what Thoreau had articulated earlier about the power of nonviolent resistance. They were simply showing the white community that they could no longer cooperate with a corrupt system. From that point on, King said, he would view Montgomery and future protest movements not as a boycott but "as an act of massive noncooperation." The success of the Montgomery campaign would confirm the validity of his theories and set off a national movement, as King and his associates were inspired to take the philosophy of passive resistance to a larger stage and confront the Jim Crow system beyond Montgomery. "After prayerful consideration, I am convinced that the psychological moment has come when a concentrated drive against injustice can bring great tangible gains," King said.

King invited sixty black ministers to gather at his father's church in Atlanta for what he described as "the first Negro Leaders Conference on Nonviolent Integration." On January 10, 1957, the group voted to form the Southern Christian Leadership Conference (SCLC) to channel the new energy that was rising among African Americans in the South. The organization's founding statement boldly proclaimed its mission to "redeem the soul of America."

Not surprisingly, Fred Shuttlesworth of Birmingham was among the most enthusiastic of the founding members, but other key names were present as well, including longtime activist Ella Baker, Methodist minister Joseph Lowery of Mobile, controversial King adviser Bayard Rustin, Baptist pastor C. K. Steele of Tallahassee, and King's closest ally in Montgomery, Ralph Abernathy. King was promptly chosen as the group's first president. Thanks to the fiery trials of Montgomery, a long-burgeoning national movement had found its leader.

Shuttlesworth said King's leadership over the organization was a given. "Dr. King was chosen because he, more than anybody else, was qualified," he recalled years later, explaining that King was the only black pastor among them at that time who had a PhD What's more, "the Montgomery protest had projected him into national prominence." But above all, said the Birmingham agitator, King was selected because "God had chosen him to be the spokesman."

4

THE ROAD TO REVOLUTION

Martin Luther King Jr.

I THINK THE THEME DR. KING WAS DEVELOPING, though certainly relevant to his time, has an even greater context than the civil rights movement or even social justice itself," Randy Woodley told me via an email exchange as I worked on this book. Woodley, a Keetoowah Cherokee pastor, teacher and activist, was among dozens of Christian leaders I reached out to as I sought to put the legacy of Martin Luther King Jr.'s Birmingham mission in context. King's message, I was reminded, spoke not just to the immediate challenges facing his African American constituency in the 1950s and 1960s, but it speaks today to other people and groups who have historically been marginalized by racial, cultural and economic oppression.

Woodley, who currently serves as professor of faith and culture at George Fox Evangelical Seminary in Portland, Oregon, as well as the school's director of Intercultural and Indigenous Studies, has worked for more than twenty-five years in ministry to Native North American communities who are still experiencing the residual effects of centuries of racial prejudice and exclusion in this nation. An unwaveringly candid and forthright activist, Woodley said Martin Luther King Jr.'s words continue to resound with penetrating relevance for today's Christians. And though he teaches King's "Letter from Birmingham Jail" to his George Fox students, he's not always sure they grasp the radical nature of what the civil rights leader was doing. "I have mostly white students at the seminary, and it is very easy for them to fantasize that they would be standing with King if given the opportunity," he said. "They idolize Dr. King without realizing the risk and suffering that was involved for the whites back then who dared cross the color line."

Evangelical moderates have lost "the spirituality of risk and doing," Woodley added. "People have fooled themselves into believing they can follow Christ and risk nothing. But to neglect to stand up for the rights of the poor and disenfranchised is not simply cowardly—it is heretical. Have we fooled ourselves into thinking that true Christian spirituality can be developed without taking the risk of losing job security, personal safety or social status?" Woodley would love to see the church recapture the "spirituality of risk" that King and his associates so brilliantly lived. "I believe we've abdicated all the admonitions in Scripture that tell us our faith is not simply what we believe but how we treat others." For Woodley, a closer examination of King's message could help us rediscover that truth.

THE THRUST OF HISTORY

Randy Woodley's words lingered in my head as I pondered the great risk involved in the mission that King embarked on as a young movement leader. King was just twenty-seven when the Montgomery campaign concluded, but by then he had already become a whirlwind media star. Though the victory was finally sealed only as a result of a federal court lawsuit, it had irreversibly launched King into the role of the symbolic figure of a brewing civil rights revolution among African Americans in the South. As this became clear to King, he appeared to embrace it—or to at least resign himself to it. "I can't stop now," he had told his congregation at Dexter Avenue Baptist after the boycott. "History has thrust something upon me from which I cannot turn away." He did, however, fret about the perils of rising to fame at such an early age. "The average man reaches this point maybe in his late forties or early fifties," he said in 1957. "But when you reach it so young, your life becomes a kind of decrescendo. You feel yourself fading from the screen at a time you should just be starting to work toward your goal."

Newspapers and magazines hailed him as "a modern Moses" and the "the greatest Negro leader since Booker T. Washington." He was invited to write for national publications and speak at major events around the nation. As the head of the Southern Christian Leadership Conference, he also was called upon by local civil rights groups throughout the South to visit their cities and recreate the kind of movement he had superintended in Montgomery. Beginning what would become his career-long custom, King rarely turned down a request. As a result the SCLC helped lead other bus boycotts in the South and began placing a special emphasis on leading campaigns to register African Americans to vote.

During this era the majority of Negroes in the South were hindered from voting through cruel and unjust local policies that made it impossible for them to meet the eligibility requirements. In some instances Negroes were met with outright threats or violence when they attempted to register. King realized early on that African Americans exercising their right to vote would be "the key to the whole solution of the South's problem."

In May 1957 King and the SCLC helped mobilize a prayer pilgrimage to Washington, D.C., where some 35,000 people assembled at the Lincoln Memorial to demand that Negroes be given the right to vote. Some six years before his "I Have a Dream" glory at the 1963 March on Washington, King's message to the crowd may not have been as soaring, but his speech, with its rhythmic refrain of "Give Us the Ballot," was unmistakably to the point and struck the right chords for that particular moment.

Over the next three years King worked tirelessly to promote this message, traveling around the country to deliver passionate speeches and lobby political leaders. Finally, in late 1959, King resigned his position at Dexter Avenue Baptist in order to devote more attention to his SCLC work. At this time, he also agreed to become copastor of his father's congregation in Atlanta, an arrangement that allowed him the freedom to expand his national work with the SCLC without the pressures of a full-time pastorate and the feelings of guilt from being away from his parishioners. One might also detect in the move a type of resolution to a critical chapter in King's relationship with his father. Now clearly a leader in his own right, King could return to Atlanta as his own man.

STUDENT LEADERS ARISE

In the early 1960s the Negro civil rights movement was gaining momentum swiftly, in part because of King's prominent voice but also because of the grassroots efforts of countless Southern men, women—and, not insignificantly, young people. On February 1, 1960, when four male students from the all-black North Carolina Agricultural and Technical State University sat down at the "whites only" counter in the Greensboro Woolworth's store to defy the local segregation laws, they set off a wave of nonviolent protests that spread among African American college students in the South like a contagion. In time, even supportive white students joined the effort.

As the first staged "sit-ins" at lunch counters grew in popularity, King was oddly not at the forefront, even though many of the students credited him for inspiring their activism. King did, however, offer counsel to the sit-in leaders whenever they contacted him. Publicly, he called the sit-ins "one of the most significant developments in the civil rights struggle" and "a glowing example of disciplined, dignified, nonviolent action against the system of segregation." Still, King remained largely on the sidelines, even as many urged his direct involvement. Instead, it was lesser-known civil rights soldiers such as Ella Baker, Jim Lawson, John Lewis and Diane Nash who drove the movement forward. "After we had started sitting in, we were surprised and delighted to hear reports of other cities joining in," said Chicagoan Diane Nash, who in 1960 was a student leader at Fisk University in Nashville. "I think we started feeling the power of the idea whose time had come."

As the sit-in phenomenon swept the nation, protests were staged at department stores, libraries, theaters. A multitude of teen and young adult students were arrested and put in jail as a result. "The movement had a way of reaching inside you and bringing out things that even you didn't know were there, such as courage," explained Nash. "When it was time to go to jail, I was much too busy to be afraid." With Ella Baker leading the way, the young sit-in movement would eventually birth the Student Nonviolent Coordinating Committee (SNCC), popularly known as "Snick." Its existence was both a tribute to the influence of King and his SCLC, as well as a rejection of its personality-centered leadership model. Baker—who would later famously insist that King was a product of the movement, not the other way around—was a critic of what she called King's "cult of personality." Instead, she advocated "a mass movement with indigenous leadership." SNCC's decidedly more confrontational and militant flavor would from the beginning exist in an uneasy alliance with the more conservative SCLC. King's initial hesitancy to cast his lot with the student protesters would lead some SNCC members to cynically refer to him as "de Lawd."

King, ever circumspect and analytical, did not immediately jump into the sit-in fray. But when he finally did, he did so unreservedly. In October 1960 he was arrested at a department store sit-in in Atlanta. Wanting to make an example of the nation's most famous protester, an unsympathetic judge sentenced King to four months behind bars without bail. Not surprisingly, King's incarceration made national headlines, and then-presidential candidate John F. Kennedy immediately called Coretta King to offer his assistance. Soon JFK's brother and campaign manager Robert F. Kennedy, a well-connected lawyer, contacted the Georgia judge who had sent King to jail. Kennedy quickly arranged for bail to be set for King, and he was soon released. When large numbers of African American cast their ballots for JFK the following month, it was clear that Kennedy's support of King helped him win the votes he needed to become President of the United States.

FREEDOM RIDERS RIDING

In 1961 the Freedom Rides, another dynamic student movement, sparked more controversy throughout the South. President Kennedy, who as a candidate had spoken out boldly in favor of civil rights, signified a new hopefulness among Negroes for an increased emphasis on racial equality. The Freedom Rides set out to put that hopefulness to the test. Coordinated by leaders from SNCC as well as the Congress of Racial Equality (CORE), a separate civil rights organization composed of black and white members, the Freedom Rides targeted segregated buses and terminals. Supreme Court rulings in 1946 and 1960 had struck down state laws that enforced segregation in interstate buses and bus terminals because such laws violated the Interstate Commerce Act, which prohibited discrimination in interstate passenger transportation. Nevertheless, in the South, Negroes were still being forced to ride in the back of interstate buses and were also restricted from using "whites only" waiting rooms and restaurants at bus terminals.

In the Freedom Rides an integrated movement of students rode interstate buses and used lunch counters and waiting rooms that were designated "whites only" in order to expose the illegal practice of segregation in those settings. The Freedom Riders elicited violent reactions from white mobs in various cities throughout the South. The Alabama cities of Anniston, Birmingham and Montgomery became flashpoints for violent clashes in which the nonviolent Freedom Riders were beaten and buses were torched. At an event in Montgomery, where King had returned to speak at his friend and SCLC associate Rev. Ralph Abernathy's church, the Freedom Riders who had come to hear King attracted a mob of angry white supremacists that tried to break into the church and threatened to burn it down. Seeking safety in the church basement, King put in a call to now Attorney General Robert Kennedy, who quickly had National Guardsmen dispatched to protect the people in the church. King later told a group of Freedom Riders that they "must develop the quiet courage of dying for a cause. We would not like to see anyone die. We all love life and there are no martyrs here. But we are well aware that we may have some casualties."

Those words were especially true for the two busloads of Freedom Riders headed to Birmingham in May 1961. The first bus was greeted by mob violence about sixty miles east of the Magic City. Raging white rioters slashed the bus's tires, smashed the windows, and tossed firebombs into the bus, smoking out its black and white passengers, who were promptly beaten by the rioters until state police arrived.

The second bus arrived in Birmingham hours later, but its Freedom Riders did not know that Commissioner Bull Connor had been tipped off regarding their plans. Eager to teach the riders a lesson, Connor arranged for the Ku Klux Klan to meet the arriving protesters and spend fifteen uninterrupted minutes with them before dispatching his officers. Dozens of angry white men soon attacked the Freedom Riders, beating several of them so severely that national news organizations descended on the area to report the fallout.

At the center of the chaos, of course, was Fred Shuttlesworth, who helped lead efforts to rescue the students and get many of them to the hospital. Shuttlesworth also managed to smuggle several of the protesters to his home for protection and first aid.

Reaching its peak during the summer of 1961, the Freedom Rides provided for the media, and by extension all of America, one more living demonstration of the heated oppression and hatred against Negroes that besieged the South. It would serve to inspire and galvanize many new recruits to the cause of civil rights, and especially to the King-flavored brand of nonviolent confrontation.

THE ALBANY COLLAPSE

Despite the visible progress of the movement, the sheer magnitude of the Deep South's "elephant" would soon reassert itself in stunning fashion. In the spring of 1962, King and the SCLC were dealt one of the most devastating setbacks of its brief existence.

In Albany, Georgia, where King and his cohort had been invited to help bolster the local black community's longstanding battle against the city's vicious program of segregation, King would encounter his first formidable challenge to his developing nonviolent methodology. The local movement had already received support from SNCC and the NAACP, but they ran into a tough and unyielding force in the form of the local authorities. The protesters employed marches, sit-ins and prayer meetings in the streets. But, in retrospect, the movement might have been seduced into a false sense of invincibility by its earlier successes. The SCLC's loose and unfocused efforts were no match for Albany police chief Laurie Pritchett, who strategically studied the methods of King's nonviolent movement and determined to counter them by departing from the anticipated script. Pritchett decided that he would not use dogs, billy clubs or any show of force. He had even put his officers through the kind of extensive training that SNCC used to prepare its student protesters, teaching them how to *not* respond during sit-ins when they were slapped or spat upon. Pritchett told his policemen, "If they do this, you will not use force. We're going to out-nonviolent them." And this, recalled Pritchett years later, is what the police department and other people did to thwart the Albany campaign.

Pritchett did not use violence, but he jailed the protesters continually for breaking minor local laws. To put it in athletic terms, he disrupted them before they could even get into the flow of their offense. King himself was arrested three times. Though the movement did wind up bankrupting the local bus company through its boycott, the overall payoff for the SCLC was minimal. The Albany authorities kept pressing with this combination of reverse nonviolence and incarceration, until the protesters were left feeling neutralized.

The campaign concluded with a whimper rather than the dramatic bang that had become expected. Still, King learned something from the experience. "I didn't understand at the time what was happening," he said later. "We lost an initiative that we never regained. We attacked the political power structure instead of the economic power structure. You don't win against a political power structure where you don't have the votes."

It was a crucial lesson that he would carry with him to his next major campaign in the equally intractable city of Birmingham.

As Birmingham Goes

Martin Luther King, Jr.

WHILE VISITING THE BIRMINGHAM CIVIL RIGHTS INSTITUTE, the brilliant museum of the movement's history located in the city's center, I was introduced to a 1961 CBS documentary chronicling the racial crisis that gripped the city during that period. The special report, called *Who Speaks for Birmingham?*, featured an assortment of black and white citizens offering their unsurprisingly polarized takes on the racial situation in their community. I learned later that the documentary grew out of a 1960 *New York Times* story by Pulitzer Prize–winning journalist Harrison Salisbury that provided a brutally vivid account of the white supremacy that cast a "reign of terror" over Birmingham's black and Jewish residents. City officials were so infuriated by the story that they filed a series of criminal libel suits against the *Times*. The suits were later dismissed by federal judges, but prior to that CBS correspondent Howard K. Smith came to town to determine whose side of the story was more accurate. As an eyewitness to the May 1961 Freedom Rides incident in Birmingham, it didn't take Smith long to figure out that Salisbury actually might've been too kind.

In the black-and-white footage from the special that plays in a continuous loop at the museum, viewers hear from a white Birmingham socialite named Eleanor Bridges who said she was not personally aware of any prejudice in Birmingham and lamented the fact that since the civil rights mentality had spread among the city's Negroes, they no longer "spontaneously break into song." John Temple Graves, a revered columnist for the *Birmingham Post-Herald*, strongly protested Salisbury's characterization of the city and insisted that Birmingham's "sins" were no worse than those of other cities in the nation. On the "black" side of the debate, Fred Shuttlesworth said he agreed with Salisbury's report "whole-heartedly" and calmly recounted the numerous occasions of beatings, bombings and arrests experienced by himself and others in the Negro community. "Life is a struggle here in Birmingham," he said, "but it's a glorious struggle." But the most poignant moment came from an unidentified high school or college student. Though her exact age is unclear, the look of overwhelming sadness and exasperation on her face is not. "I can tell the people of America, don't live here," she tells the CBS reporter. "White, black, red, yellow, green. Not under this. Life isn't worth living."

Thanks to national media, the world was treated to increasingly disturbing examples of the African American experience in Birmingham.

BODIES AND SOULS

By the 1960s, nearly 40 percent of Birmingham's 350,000 residents were African American. Since the 1940s, moderate voices in the community had tried to build bridges between blacks and whites, but with little lasting success.

In fact, class divisions among black Birminghamians were at times just as problematic for racial progress as the rift between blacks and whites. Those Birmingham blacks who had "made it," as it were, typically occupied the professional ranks—doctors, lawyers, teachers and ministers. Having overcome major barriers to succeed, they often looked down on the working-class population. At the same time, they were cognizant of the injustices that kept most blacks "bottled in the slums and restricted to the blighted areas" of Birmingham, though they were usually reluctant say so in a public way. While this led some in the black community to disparage their wealthier neighbors as "bourgeois" Negroes or "Uncle Toms," the politics of their respective identities in the city were more complex. For black professionals to speak out on civil rights was a tricky proposition. This was still the South, after all, and deep down they understood the tenuous nature of their success in the city.

The conservative businessman Arthur (A. G.) Gaston was a prime example of the delicate duality that fell upon many in the black middle class. He had become a millionaire through his insurance business and other ventures, including a bank, motel and funeral home. Having built a reputation before white Birmingham as the city's preeminent black leader by presenting himself as a conciliatory figure, his clout proffered him a unique standing in the community. But quietly, Gaston funded Shuttlesworth and the work of the Alabama Christian Movement for Human Rights. Other middle-class black Birminghamians fell into this same category of surreptitious civil rights support.

One thing that everyone in the African American community agreed on, however, was that the attacks against the Freedom Riders—and Bull Connor's role in them—were an atrocity. The city was governed by a commission model, and its three officers, including Connor, were each promoters of hard line segregationist policies. But after the Klan, in cahoots with the local authorities, waged their vicious assault on the Freedom Riders, Birmingham's middle-class blacks, as well as its white moderates, had had enough. In early 1963 citizens voted out the old commission form of government in favor of an office of mayor, effectively stripping Connor of his power. Winning the mayoral election was Albert

Boutwell, a former segregationist who had run as a relative moderate (for Birmingham) on racial issues. Connor's days were numbered, but before giving up his power, he held on through a legal battle that kept him in office long enough to serve as a prop for a long-proposed Birmingham campaign.

After months of demonstrations and arrests failed to accomplish the goals of the Albany campaign in 1962, many in the media and even within the civil rights ranks pronounced nonviolent resistance "a dead issue." As a result, Martin Luther King Jr. was eager to demonstrate to the naysayers that his preferred form of protest was still an effective answer to the ugly system of injustice and discrimination that faced Negroes in the South. He needed a battlefield that would be the ideal location to prove that his ideas—and by extension that *he*—were still relevant. What was the most impenetrable city in the South? That was an easy one. King and his SCLC deputies knew it was Birmingham.

Fred Shuttlesworth had pastored Birmingham's Bethel Baptist Church for eight years, but now both he and his congregation were beginning to feel restless with one another. In June 1961, after years of beatings, bombings and harassment by both the police and the Klan, he decided to accept a pastorate at Revelation Missionary Baptist Church in Cincinnati, Ohio. It was a difficult decision for the Birmingham radical, who was as fiercely determined as ever to bring down the city's segregationist system and lead its black citizens to freedom. However, after weeks of agonizing prayer, he realized a move to the safer environs of the North (as well as the larger paycheck that came with it) might be the best thing for his growing family. Still, even though he was moving four hundred miles away, Shuttlesworth vowed to continue leading the ACMHR, and he did just that, driving back to Alabama every other week to continue his fearless agitating. The "Wild Man from Birmingham" could not stay away from his city when the work there was unfinished.

As a founding member of the SCLC, Shuttlesworth had been beseeching the organization to stage a campaign in Birmingham for years. Early on as head of the SCLC, Martin Luther King's hesitancy to go to Birmingham and other major hotspots had as much to do with his juggling act of leading a national movement while pastoring Dexter Avenue Baptist as it did with his excessive caution. But after his return to Atlanta, King's foot-dragging became more a sign of his proclivity for overthinking a matter. This trait had led to earlier disagreements with Shuttlesworth, whose blunt style clashed with King's circumspection. Biographer Andrew Manis recounts a revealing incident that occurred when Shuttlesworth differed strongly with King and Ralph Abernathy over the nature of Christ's resurrection, which King and Abernathy speculated could have been "an image or apparition" rather than a literal bodily appearance. Shuttlesworth, a no-nonsense biblicist, understood their suggestion as an expression of doubt regarding the historical account and told them as much: "If God lied about that, he lied about everything else," he said. Years later, Shuttlesworth shared that he didn't think King actually disbelieved the resurrection but that his theorizing was a reflection of the Atlanta preacher's penchant for theological contemplation. Shuttlesworth, on the other hand, did not allow room for such intellectual musing in his worldview. King knew after that encounter never to debate doctrine with his Birmingham colleague again. But even if King was disinclined to engage Shuttlesworth on theological matters, he had no choice but to respect him for his courageous leadership in Birmingham. So, he listened whenever Shuttlesworth raised the idea of a campaign in the South's most daunting city. But listen was all he did.

Shuttlesworth, who had grown weary of King's indecision, continued to hammer the issue. He recognized a providential opening following the debacle in Albany. "Coming out of Albany, Dr. King's image was slightly on the wane," he recalled years later. "The SCLC needed a victory." Shuttlesworth once again invited King and his SCLC team to deploy in Birmingham and help the city's black community confront segregation "with our bodies and souls." He told them, "Birmingham is where it's at, gentlemen. I assure you, if you come to Birmingham, we will not only gain prestige but really shake the country." Shuttlesworth truly believed that "as Birmingham goes, so goes the nation." After some initial reluctance, King finally agreed.

PROJECT CONFRONTATION

King and his SCLC deputies descended on Birmingham with a carefully crafted battle plan. They were determined not to repeat any of the mistakes made in Albany. "After Albany, Dr. King decided he wasn't going into any situation again where he was not in control," remembers then-SCLC executive director Wyatt Tee Walker. "The most valuable lesson we learned from Albany was that our targets were too numerous. We diluted our strength by going after everything that was segregated. Up to that time we had been trying to win the hearts of white southerners, and that was a mistake, a misjudgment. We realized that you had to hit them in the pocket."

Walker drew up a plan that he called "Project C" for "Confrontation." The movement decided to take direct aim at Birmingham's economic system. During the Easter season of 1963, they would boycott downtown stores and eateries with Jim Crow policies. In addition, they planned to gradually roll out a series of sit-ins, kneel-ins and marches. The SCLC's four demands included desegregation of all public facilities and department stores, the hiring of blacks in sales and clerical positions, the release of jailed demonstrators, and the establishment of an official biracial committee to address the community's race problems.

The campaign launched in earnest on the morning of April 3, 1963, when twenty-four college students staged sit-ins at four downtown lunch counters. Rather than create a scene with mass arrests, the businesses all closed in response. Two days later, on Palm Sunday, protesters on the way to city hall were arrested. The protesters stuck to the plan, but the demonstrations were unremarkable at best.

Initially, Bull Connor exercised the same kind of restraint as Police Chief Laurie Pritchett of Albany. He did not use violence, and protesters were promptly arrested. But as the jails began to fill up, Connor needed another weapon to deter demonstrators. On April 10 the city got a court injunction that forbade public demonstrations in the city. In the past King had avoided breaking actual court orders, focusing instead on the illegal restrictions put in place by local municipalities. But this time he felt he needed to make an exception or the campaign might wither. Memories of Albany filled his mind. But there was another problem. The SCLC was running low on funds that could be used for bail money. The leaders were desperate for King to return to his national speaking schedule to help replenish the coffers. If they didn't, at least three hundred protesters might wind up stranded behind bars in the Birmingham jail.

RESERVATIONS AND REVELATIONS

King was caught at an impasse. If he didn't return to the speaking circuit, he might endanger the future of the larger movement; however, if he left the city now, it would likely ensure another colossal failure. Furthermore, King's associates knew that if he stayed, he planned to defy the court order and be arrested. That would deal an unquestionably devastating blow to the movement's short-term survival. "If you go to jail, we are lost," one aide argued. "The battle of Birmingham is lost. We need a lot of money. We need it now. You are the only one who has the contacts to get it." What's more, Daddy King was concerned that if Martin went to jail in a vicious

city such as Birmingham, where the cops were in collusion with
the Klan, there might be a good chance that he would wind up
murdered behind bars. However, if King did not go to jail, while
hundreds of others had before him, his leadership would be dimin-
ished and he would have failed thousands who had put their hopes
in his presence there in Magic City.

On the morning of April 12, Good Friday, King sat at the SCLC's
Birmingham headquarters, room 30 of the Gaston Motel. Surrounded by twenty-four of his team members (including the
group's highest-ranking woman, Dorothy Cotton), he listened pensively as the leaders discussed the predicament before them. As
they talked, King later said, "a sense of doom began to pervade the
room." He looked around him and saw that his most committed
leaders appeared "overwhelmed by a feeling of hopelessness" for
the first time in their work together.

Saying he needed to pray alone, King retreated to an adjoining
room. There he stood in the middle of the floor by himself. At that
moment, King felt he was "standing at the center of all that my life
had brought me to be." He thought about the twenty-four people
waiting in the next room, the three hundred people waiting in jail,
and the long-suffering Negro community in Birmingham. Finally,
he thought of "the twenty million black people" in America "who
dreamed that someday they might be able to cross the Red Sea of
injustice and find their way into the promised land of integration
and freedom." Then it all became clear. Thirty minutes later, King
returned to his colleagues in room 30 dressed in a denim shirt and
jeans. "I don't know what will happen. I don't know where the
money will come from, but I have to make a faith act," he said.
"I've got to march." King asked Ralph Abernathy to join him, and
he agreed. Then, King recalled, "we all linked hands involuntarily,
almost as if there had been some divine signal, and twenty-five
voices in Room 30 at the Gaston Motel in Birmingham, Alabama,

chanted the battle hymn of our movement, 'We Shall Overcome.'"

That afternoon, following a mass meeting at Sixteenth Street Baptist Church, just across the way from the Gaston Motel, King and Abernathy set out on their fateful march, headed north toward city hall. Thanks to the injunction the demonstrations stayed small—only about forty other marchers joined King and Abernathy. They had only walked a few blocks when they ran into a blockade of Connor's men. In a departure from the nonviolent approach the police had applied up until then, one of the cops, in a burst of rage, grabbed King by the back of his belt, yanked him off his feet, and forcefully tossed him into the back of a police van.

King, Abernathy and the other marchers were taken to the city jail, where King was promptly separated from the others and thrown into solitary confinement.

Eight White Preachers, or With Friends Like These

We do not believe that these days of new hope
are days when extreme measures are
justified in Birmingham.

PUBLIC STATEMENT BY
THE ALABAMA CLERGYMEN

Martin Luther King Jr.

THERE'S A RECURRING THEME that I've observed—and personally experienced—in the interaction between black and white Christian leaders in America. In fact, I'm thinking this dynamic could apply to the relationship between any minority and majority group, but my predominant experience with it has come in the context of black and white leadership in evangelical Christian settings. So, I'll engage it from that perspective.

It goes something like this.

A black (minority) Christian leader is identified by white (majority) Christian leaders as a rising star and someone who shares their values, mission and commitment to the gospel. The white Christian leaders recruit the black leader, mentor and groom him, and at the right time elevate him to a position of authority in an organization where that black leader is typically "the first" black man (or woman) to hold that particular role. It's an inspirational narrative and one that usually gives us a glimmer of hope about the progress of racial reconciliation in American Christianity.

On the very day that I'm writing this chapter, in fact, it was announced that the Southern Baptist Convention, a denomination founded in part as a way of defending the institution of slavery in the antebellum South, had elected New Orleans pastor Fred Luter as its first African American president. This historic development did not go unnoticed by the mainstream press, either. *The New York Times*, NPR and a slew of other media chimed in with reports about the significance of Luter's achievement—which, I suppose, is a sign both of how far we've come and of how far behind some perceive us to be.

Mixed in with the celebratory reactions to the SBC's milestone were a number of sobering voices cautioning against reading too much into Luter's election. "Unfortunately, the president of the convention controls no budget, no personnel," said Rev. Dwight McKissic, an influential Arlington, Texas, pastor whose blog routinely charts the racial happenings in the SBC. "[The SBC presidency] has influence, but it has no real inherent authority or power. The jury is still out, but we'll see when they get ready to hire an entity head whether or not they're serious."

McKissic's "they," it appears, was a reference to the white executive leadership of the denomination—you know, the folks who *really* run the operation. And so, it would appear, even when a black man rises to the very top of an evangelical institution, he's still not in charge. This is both the perception and reality experienced by many people of color in predominantly white organizations.

It's a disheartening sequel to the "black-white Christian leadership" storyline. And it essentially reflects the power dynamic between majority and minority stakeholders: those who have historically possessed the most capital and have been in charge the longest ultimately will call the shots. Therefore, black leaders who are elevated to positions of power in predominantly white Christian organizations function more as symbols than as genuine "there's a new sheriff in town" powerbrokers. And these leaders are typically bound for frustration.

BEWARE OF ROSA PARKS

In my 2006 book, *Reconciliation Blues*, I spent an entire chapter rehearsing the stories of trailblazing African American leaders who rose to significant heights in evangelical organizations only to discover that their interpretation of empowerment did not necessarily match up with the ideas of their white superiors. One of those leaders was Rev. Jerald January. Currently the senior pastor of Vernon Park Church of God, a large congregation on Chicago's South Side, Jerald served in a variety of church and parachurch leadership roles before being named the president of a major Christian relief organization in the 1990s. In that position he achieved great notoriety and acclaim. He was responsible for all aspects of the group's national operations. He spoke at conferences and events around the nation. HarperCollins published his autobiography, *A Messed-Up Ride or a Dressed Up Walk*. It's probably accurate to say he was the highest-ranking African American leader of a major white evangelical organization up to that time.

But it was not to last.

Jerald told me, "The fact of the matter is that African American males usually last four years or less in management or upper-management positions at evangelical organizations. That's about as long as it goes."

His explanation for the limited shelf life of black men in leadership at evangelical institutions suggested an amalgamation of standard workplace conflict and unspoken racial tension. Sadly, in many of these situations, the two are often indistinguishable.

Jerald said he was the "flavor of the month" for a brief period, but then the luster began to wear off and he was left trying to run a huge nonprofit without buy-in or support from many of his key colleagues. "I wasn't trying to make trouble," he told me. "I was just there to do my job. But people will read into what you do out of their own fears and insecurities." After running into repeated roadblocks, Jerald realized being "the first" wasn't as special as he'd thought.

The final straw occurred after Jerald had mined his numerous church contacts to secure Rosa Parks as a keynote speaker for a major fundraising banquet. He just knew he'd hit a home run, and the community was indeed excited about the announcement of the legendary civil rights matriarch's participation. Everyone in the organization was thrilled too—at least until a few weeks prior to the banquet. That's when Jerald was blindsided by a call from the organization's board informing him they were pulling the plug on the event. Apparently, after much discussion, they'd decided Rosa Parks might be considered "too liberal" for some of their white donors. "They were worried that she didn't seem to come from an evangelical background," Jerald explained. In other words, it was an economic decision wrapped in theological packaging.

In the years following the publication of *Reconciliation Blues*, I encountered a slew of similar stories from men and women around the country. Stories of how lofty professional titles were bestowed but true authority withheld, how diversity in leadership was applauded until someone attempted to translate that diversity into actual policy, how the "urban missions" budget lines were always the first to be cut, how elder boards were hesitant to hire nonwhite senior pastors for fear it might paint them as an "ethnic" church.

Jerald January's story resonated with me because I had also felt the pangs of being a solitary African American at white evangelical outfits. Looking back, the most frustrating thing was sometimes not knowing whether an issue was racial or just plain-old workplace drama. Was I jumping to conclusions to assume that something was race-related? Was I being naive to sometimes think that it wasn't? Perhaps this is part of what W. E. B. Du Bois was talking about in 1903 when he wrote about the maddening phenomenon of the Negro's "double consciousness."

DR. KING'S WHITE NOISE

Over time, many individuals I've spoken to have become convinced that people of color in leadership roles at evangelical institutions are not there to stretch the status quo by bringing their own unique perspectives to bear, but to serve as an example of how a nonwhite leader can embody and thus validate the existing white model. "It's assimilation over reconciliation," remarked one frustrated leader in an email, "the maintenance of a traditional system over the transformation of an organizational vision." If major change is to come, the white Christian gatekeepers seem to routinely insist, it must be pursued incrementally—which really is another way of saying "don't rock the boat."

In a way, this is the kind of static that Dr. King faced when he decided to bring his campaign of nonviolent resistance to Birmingham.

Granted, King's circumstances were somewhat different. He was the head of a multiracial but predominantly black organization, and therefore not accountable to any white bosses (save for the governors, mayors and police commissioners who regularly opposed him), so his was ultimately the final word on major decisions. Still, as perhaps the most-watched black man of the day, Dr. King was acutely aware of his role as a symbol. He knew his words and actions would shape and inform the opinions of millions of white Americans regarding the merit and worth of all Negroes in this country who desired their full rights as United States citizens—in fact, he counted on it.

As a result, King was conscious of his need to collaborate with sympathetic whites, especially those who identified themselves as people of faith and with whom he presumably shared a common commitment to the values of peace and reconciliation. Men such as Stanley Levison and Tom Offenburger held key advisory roles in the SCLC. And his friendships with white clergymen such as Robert Graetz in Montgomery, Joseph Ellwanger in Birmingham, Richard John Neuhaus and Abraham Joshua Heschel in later marches, and even Billy Graham (in the earlier years of King's work) reflected King's openness to interracial and interdenominational alliances.

But as the campaign in Birmingham geared up, King probably wished he had a few more white friends to lean on. He certainly wasn't getting any love from the white press. The local *Birmingham News*, a consistent critic of the civil rights movement, was no fan of King's arrival in town. Nationally, *Time* magazine criticized King's campaign as a "poorly timed protest," while *Newsweek* portrayed King and his nemesis Bull Connor as equal and opposite extremists. The *Washington Post* described King's demonstrations as "of doubtful utility," and, pointing to the election of the moderate mayoral candidate Albert Boutwell as a hopeful sign, both the *Post* and *New York Times* opined that King and his followers should exercise more patience and wait for the political process to bring the needed change.

King, however, was convinced such editorializing was shortsighted and at once disconnected from the lived experiences of the African Americans who were advocating for their rights. As King would later observe, "[The national press] did not realize that it was ridiculous to speak of timing when the clock of history showed that the Negro had already suffered one hundred years of delay."

But it wasn't just the press calling King's timing into question. President Kennedy and U.S. Attorney General Robert Kennedy urged King to wait. And Billy Graham, who had praised the movement's success in Montgomery, suggested that his "good personal friend" might be stoking the racial tension in Birmingham by moving too fast and that he should "put the brakes on a little bit." Graham added, "What I would like to see now is a period of quietness in which moderation prevails."

This idea of "moderation" grew to be the prevalent theme of the day, one that haunted the civil rights movement in the same way that King later said the words "bad timing" became "ghosts haunting our every move in Birmingham." It's no wonder that King would be compelled to title his 1964 book about the campaign *Why We Can't Wait*.

THERE WERE BLACK CRITICS TOO

King was not immune to criticisms from the black community, either. Many traditional black leaders also adopted a more moderate stance, especially those like A. G. Gaston who owned businesses or who had attained a relatively comfortable standard of life in Birmingham. For them, King's presence as an interloping agitator represented a potential threat to their hard-earned achievements in the community, because it could falsely communicate the idea that *all* of the city's African Americans were siding with King. Emory O. Jackson, the editor of the black newspaper the *Birmingham World*, labeled King's direct-action campaigns as "both wasteful and worthless" and advised restraint by all parties. While Jackson strongly opposed racial segregation, he believed the court system was the most effective arena for challenging it. Consequently, the *World* played down coverage of the protests.

Gaston, a member of the Birmingham Chamber of Commerce, frowned on the campaign even as he lent it his support. The local mogul opened the doors of his Gaston Motel to provide lodging to King and the visiting SCLC members from Atlanta and Montgomery, while at the same time criticizing their tactics. His complicated juggling act as a black civic leader was, in some ways, just as crucial to the movement as Shuttleworth's brazen activism. "I was with the movement, but my idea of approaching it was somewhat different from some of the folks that you might call radical," Gaston would later say. "My place on the chamber there got some of the [white] leaders to move. They were willing to do some things for me that they wouldn't have done for Martin King or Shuttlesworth."

THE BIRMINGHAM EIGHT

King encountered no shortage of opposition to his Birmingham mission, but by far the most significant critique of "Project C" would come from eight white men who were members of King's own vocational field. The ministers came from largely white religious affiliations and led segregated congregations, but their liberal views on race relations and social concerns had garnered them that vague but telling label of "moderate."

In January 1963 the state of Alabama witnessed the inauguration of Governor George Wallace, whose scary inaugural rant "segregation now, segregation tomorrow, segregation forever" became a rallying cry for segregationists across the South. Disturbed by Wallace's speech, the eight ministers joined other Alabama clergy in issuing a joint public statement calling for the dignity of all people. "Every human being is created in the image of God," they asserted, "and is entitled to respect as a fellow human being with all basic rights, privileges, and responsibilities which belong to humanity." In the wake of Wallace's incendiary address, the ministers' "Law and Order" statement sought to point Alabama's citizens to the importance of adhering to the laws of the land, even as divisive court decisions promised an imminent reality of desegregation of the state's public schools and colleges. Not surprisingly, the reviews were mixed.

If a way of testing someone's "moderate" street cred is by measuring the amount of grief he or she receives from either side of the spectrum, then these clergy earned the moniker legitimately. After the January statement, death threats and charges of "communists," "nigger lovers" and "integrationists" flew their way like flaming lawn darts. But these would pale in comparison to the legacy they were about to cement for themselves when, three months later, they decided to release another public statement, this time taking to task the MLK-led campaign that had invaded their city. Like others in Birmingham, the eight ministers were convinced that the best hope for their city resided in the election of Albert Boutwell, a fellow moderate they felt should be given a chance to turn things around gradually. King's movement, however, did not come to Birmingham to wait.

The white clergymen's joint statement regarding the demonstrations was composed on April 12, 1963—the same day that King and his chief deputy, Ralph Abernathy, were arrested and locked in the city jail. The statement was published in both of the city's newspapers the following day. The letter, in effect, functioned as both a proclamation and a rebuke. It did not mention King by name, but the intimation was clear:

> We the undersigned clergymen are among those who, in January, issued "an appeal for law and order and common sense," in dealing with racial problems in Alabama. We expressed understanding that honest convictions in racial matters could properly be pursued in the courts, but urged that decisions of those courts should in the meantime be peacefully obeyed.
>
> Since that time there had been some evidence of increased forbearance and a willingness to face facts. Responsible citizens have undertaken to work on various problems which cause racial friction and unrest. In Birmingham, recent public events have given indication that

we all have opportunity for a new constructive and realistic approach to racial problems.

However, we are now confronted by a series of demonstrations by some of our Negro citizens, directed and led in part by outsiders. We recognize the natural impatience of people who feel that their hopes are slow in being realized. But we are convinced that these demonstrations are unwise and untimely.

We agree rather with certain local Negro leadership which has called for honest and open negotiation of racial issues in our area. And we believe this kind of facing of issues can best be accomplished by citizens of our own metropolitan area, white and Negro, meeting with their knowledge and experience of the local situation. All of us need to face that responsibility and find proper channels for its accomplishment.

Just as we formerly pointed out that "hatred and violence have no sanction in our religious and political traditions," we also point out that such actions as incite to hatred and violence, however technically peaceful those actions may be, have not contributed to the resolution of our local problems. We do not believe that these days of new hope are days when extreme measures are justified in Birmingham.

We commend the community as a whole, and the local news media and law enforcement officials in particular, on the calm manner in which these demonstrations have been handled. We urge the public to continue to show restraint should the demonstrations continue, and the law enforcement officials to remain calm and continue to protect our city from violence.

We further strongly urge our own Negro community to withdraw support from these demonstrations, and to unite locally in working peacefully for a better Birmingham. When rights are consistently denied, a cause should be pressed in the courts and in negotiations among local leaders, and not in the streets. We appeal to both our white and Negro citizenry to observe the principles of law and order and common sense.

Bishop C. C. J. Carpenter, D.D., LL.D., Episcopalian Bishop of Alabama
Bishop Joseph A. Durick, D.D., Auxiliary Bishop, Roman Catholic Diocese
    of Mobile, Birmingham

Rabbi Milton L. Grafman, Temple Emanu-El, Birmingham, Alabama

Bishop Paul Hardin, Methodist Bishop of the Alabama-West Florida Conference

Bishop Nolan B. Harmon, Bishop of the North Alabama Conference of the Methodist Church

Rev. George M. Murray, D.D., LL.D, Bishop Coadjutor, Episcopal Diocese of Alabama

Rev. Edward V. Ramage, Moderator, Synod of the Alabama Presbyterian Church in the United States

Rev. Earl Stallings, Pastor, First Baptist Church, Birmingham, Alabama

Their names are not familiar now, but the eight ministers were each influential and respected in their corners of Birmingham, and were among some of the most prominent religious leaders in the state of Alabama during that time. They weren't just local pastors but regional bishops and national officers of their denominations. So, for them to add their names to such a document made a statement. Though they were all technically "moderates," the eight white clergy represented a sundry collection of social philosophies and religious expressions. Still, they found unity around the belief that demonstrations like King's would only lead to hostility, violence and further civil unrest. This, of course, was exactly what King and his associates desired to bring to the surface for all of America to see. The eight ministers urged patience and restraint; Project C was designed to capitalize on impatience and frustration.

COLLIDING WITH KING

Reading the eight ministers' statement today reveals much about the confusing times in which it was composed and the differences between white and black perspectives on the racial situation in the South. The white clergy, for instance, placed confidence in the judicial system and the Birmingham police, which would have been a stretch for many African Americans given the way those institutions had regarded (or disregarded) them and their concerns in the past. Consequently, the ministers' statement occasionally fell into a paternalistic voice that appeared insensitive to the painful reality of the Negro plight in Birmingham at the time. It's because of this, as well as Dr. King's forthcoming response, that many who read the statement now might peg the signatories as racists, at worst, or white religious snobs, at best. Unfortunately, reading the statement with this mindset can be unfair both to the ministers and to the complex environment in which they were operating.

In *Blessed Are the Peacemakers*, his excellent chronicle of the eight white clergymen's lives before and after their intellectual collision with King, historian S. Jonathan Bass provides an astute comparison between the sometimes contradictory philosophies and goals of the white clergy and King's movement:

> SCLC preachers wanted extensive press coverage of the crisis to reveal southern injustice, to raise money, and to create national pressure to force local change. The white ministers hoped the national media would ignore the city. As King fasted that Good Friday before his march to jail, the white religious leaders ate lunch. The black ministers stayed at the only lodging available to them, the Gaston Motel; the white clergy met at the finest hotel in Birmingham. The Birmingham clergy desired to end the demonstrations; King wanted them to continue. King believed the quest for civil rights should be contested in the streets. The white religious leaders hoped to see the cause pursued gradually, in the court system.

Where Bass's tome is most helpful, though, is in its humanization of the eight ministers, who paid a high price for both their commitment to racial equality and their opposition to King's disruptive tactics. Today, the eight men serve as little more than symbols, historical foils in the "Birmingham" chapter of the Martin Luther King Jr. narrative. Indeed, even in 1963, King clearly viewed their letter more as a steppingstone for getting across his own message than as a human document from a group of three-dimensional spiritual leaders.

But the Birmingham Eight were more than symbols, more than props. The eight clergymen, writes Bass, "were a curious blend of liberal intellectuals, conservative theologians, Social Gospel advocates, revivalists, reformers, and Calvinists." Similar to King, most of the men had ministry in their blood "as the sons and grandsons" of preachers and religious activists. Ranging from their forties to early seventies, the group members had real generational differences that affected their views on race relations. Yet they shared a common purpose as spiritual leaders.

In his interaction with the eight, Bass reveals men who occupied different points on the "moderate" spectrum—some who were more staunchly gradualist and others who were more bent toward the radical. Though clearly creatures of their time, they cared deeply about social justice, the welfare of their city and state, and the future of their nation. Bishop Durick and Rabbi Grafman, as leaders of Birmingham's Catholic and Jewish communities respectively, were both familiar with the presence of local prejudice against their non-Protestant faiths and worked tirelessly to counter it. But while advocating for social change, the eight clergymen were also devoted to serving the needs of their parishioners and keeping the peace in their immediate community. In short, in addition to being public intellectuals, they were local pastors who had to keep in mind the attitudes and interests of their congregations as well as their own professional livelihoods. And in the South at that time, this meant a minister was required to navigate the delicate racial tripwires of the day.

In addition to risking a reduction in their membership rolls, white clergy who spoke out on racial issues could also draw the ire of hardcore segregationists who took it upon themselves to "straighten out" white ministers who preached suspicious-sounding sermons about "unity" and "the brotherhood of man." This kind of thing could get a pastor chased out of town—or worse.

It was no small gesture, then, for a group of white Southern clergymen to raise their voices, even at a moderate level, and occupy the office of public prophet the best way they knew how.

The mixture of social perspectives possessed by the Birmingham Eight, and their varied responses to the issues facing them, reflect the views owned by some Christians today when it comes to addressing the sticky problems of race, privilege and power in today's faith-based settings. At the risk of overgeneralizing, I'll suggest that the eight ministers comprise three key classifications on the "Christian moderate" continuum. And if we inspect each one closely enough, we might very well recognize our own viewpoints and experiences among them:

The über-gradualists. A conservative perspective highlighted by an elitist brand of compassion that, according to Bass, "actively pursued opportunities to aid southern blacks in social progress, but only within the framework of segregation." In this view, blacks were still inferior to whites; however, they needed Christian love in spite of their lower estate. Bishops Carpenter and Harmon, both in their seventies and the eldest members of the group, represent this paternalistic position that often vacillated between supporting civil rights for blacks and defending the segregated status quo.

The meta-moderates. An ostensibly progressive position that advocates for a socially active Christianity, but only within the context of current laws and injunctions. Bishops Durick, Hardin and Murray, along with Rabbi Grafman, embraced this approach, which Bass characterizes as neither "integrationist" nor "segregationist" but *de*-segregationist. "I am convinced on Christian and patriotic grounds that I must oppose racial discrimination and injustice," Murray said. However, Murray and his meta-moderate colleagues drew the line at using King's strategy of civil disobedience, which they viewed as "extreme." Unlike the Atlanta preacher, they were confident that, in time, the federal judiciary's advocacy of civil rights would make the difference. Therefore, for them, civil disobedience should only be used as a method of last resort.

The reluctant radicals. When black demonstrators quietly showed up on Easter Sunday 1963 to attend services at First Presbyterian and First Baptist, Reverends Ramage and Stallings were thrust into the thorny position of either extending Christian hospitality to their guests or letting it be known that Negroes—especially protesters operating under the pretense of being Sunday morning worshipers—were not welcome. Over the objections of the clamorous segregationists sprinkled throughout their congregations, both Ramage and Stallings took a principled stance and chose Christian love over racist belligerence. But it cost them. Theirs is perhaps the most tragic position of all, for reluctant radicals by definition pay a price for their adherence to a socially progressive perspective. In the case of Ramage and Stallings, it wasn't even their intention to stir the pot of integration in Birmingham. The issue, however, had literally shown up on their doorsteps. Confronted head-on, they sensed no other option but to do the "Christian" thing. (In King's Birmingham epistle, Stallings even garnered a personal shout-out from the civil rights leader for allowing black visitors to worship at First Baptist on a nonsegregated basis. He was the only member of the Birmingham Eight to be mentioned by name—but that too would only add to his problems.) Even as their parishioners conspired against them and demanded they revise the open-door policy of their respective congregations to keep Negroes out, Ramage and Stallings stood their ground and were eventually forced out as a result. Says Bass, "Unlike so many white southern ministers, Ramage and Stallings had chosen to act as spiritual leaders rather than social followers." They did so to their own peril.

Living during one of the most tumultuous and uncertain periods in our nation's history, the Birmingham Eight had no finished blueprint for how to be faithful and courageous in the face of rancorous and often deadly racial division. They were at least four months away from hearing "I Have a Dream" for the first time, and, as it would turn out, several weeks away from the first appearance of King's "Letter from Birmingham Jail." That the white clergymen's measured yet earnest steps toward reconciliation and justice would be flipped around and used against them for the purpose of, well, reconciliation and justice may be one of the greatest ironies of the civil rights movement. Moreover, it was a staggering demonstration of Martin Luther King Jr.'s single-minded brilliance and resolve.

An Angry Dr. King

Martin Luther King Jr.

In the 2012 hit superhero film *The Avengers,* a serpent-like, mechanical behemoth is closing in on our ragtag team of heroes. Tired and overmatched, their only hope lies hidden within the mild-mannered frame of scientist Dr. Bruce Banner, who morphs into the big, green and powerful creature known as the Hulk when rattled by conditions of great stress or anger. Seconds before Banner gives himself over to the rage that transforms him into his alter ego, a no-nonsense Captain America volunteers, "Dr. Banner, I think now might be a good time for you to get angry." Banner responds with a roguish smile, "That's my secret, Cap. I'm always angry."

I'm always angry.

I identified with that line and repeated it many times in the weeks after I saw the movie, much to my wife's chagrin. What resonated with me was that sense of living with a concealed, low-temperature rage; of wanting to avoid difficult people or awkward situations but being dragged into them wholesale nonetheless; of knowing certain conversations with certain folks would invariably lead to unpleasant debates about politics, religion or—heaven forbid—race, but being sucked in anyway; of being looked upon as the harmless black guy my white friends could talk to about virtually anything related to race and know they wouldn't be unfairly judged. Of course, these are all good things in their own way—sometimes it's beneficial to be dragged into uncomfortable situations or forced into interacting with people with whom we wouldn't ordinarily connect; sometimes a fierce debate on a taboo subject such as politics or religion can help both parties see a different side to an issue; sometimes being a person's nonjudgmental bridge to another cultural perspective can be viewed as an act of compassion and service. I know all that. But sometimes a man gets tired of wearing that façade Paul Laurence Dunbar spoke of so eloquently, and he just wants to detonate. Sometimes the life of constant smiling and pretending and interpreting can wear on the nerves.

I doubt I'll ever be mistaken for an Angry Black Man—a label some white critics have pinned on controversial black personalities such as Spike Lee, Jesse Jackson or Jeremiah Wright—but my wife can testify that there have been moments when I've let my guard down and regretted it. It has happened in the form of a cynical comment on Facebook, a terse email, a sarcastic comment that I never should've allowed to escape from my brain to find audible expression for others to hear.

On the other hand, it's important to talk about the harder aspects of race and culture honestly before they boil over into something destructive. This is the conclusion that an academic researcher recently arrived at through her work on race and mental health in African American men. In her study, University of North Carolina at Chapel Hill psychologist Wizdom Powell Hammond examined the phenomenon scholars call "everyday racism," which is evidenced not so much by the egregiousness of the discrimination encountered, but by its persistence and subtlety.

"These daily hassles have consequences for men's health," Hammond said. "It chips away at people's sense of humanity and very likely at their hope and optimism."

Hammond found that black men who openly discuss their everyday struggles with racial issues are less likely to suffer depression than those who keep their feelings bottled inside. This is probably Psychology 101–level stuff that applies to anyone who's repressing heavy emotions of whatever variety, but I was still fascinated to see scientific research that actually quantifies many of the things I'd experienced personally and encountered anecdotally through my work as a journalist.

And this sense of racial anxiety isn't just experienced by people of color alone; many whites know the pangs of a simmering rage and resentment as well. We hear it all the time now from the provocative voices of talk radio, the Internet and Fox News. They're as mad as hell and eager to tell you about it. They're mad at government programs that abet unworthy individuals in moving to the head of the line based strictly on their skin color or ethnicity; they're incensed over lax policies that would allow foreigners to enter this country illegally and benefit from its resources; they're disgusted by welfare-loving baby-mamas whose lifestyles appear to normalize dysfunctional behavior. But lately, what seems to irk them the most is the notion of being falsely accused of racism when we live in a country that overcame its racial hang-ups long ago. To their way of thinking, the only racists left in the world are people of color who are relentlessly screaming racism. Consequently, it sometimes seems, one of the most dangerous things for a black man to talk about today in the open air is anything related to race. Do it and risk the scorn of a tacit movement designed to squelch the idea that race still matters. One commentator even dared to put a label on the phenomenon. "You might call these people anti-anti-racists," wrote journalist Michelle Goldberg in 2012. "They are determined to push back against any narrative that would suggest that a black man has been targeted for the color of his skin."

In the end it all comes back to anger—anger at injustice, anger at what we perceive to be injustice, anger at not being able to speak frankly about those real and perceived injustices.

Is it any wonder, then, that many of us are always angry?

ANGRY ROOTS SHOWING

I mentioned earlier how frustrated I became after that traffic-cop incident in Atlanta, where the historical ghosts of the Deep South setting and the feeling that I was being treated as little more than a racial statistic (rather than a human being lost in an unfamiliar part of town) conspired to test my Christian charity. My friend LaTonya is a kind and unassuming woman in her early thirties who you'd never guess possesses a piercing wit. She jokes that whenever she's preparing to visit the South, she gets "pre-annoyed" simply as an act of solidarity with her black ancestors who suffered under Jim Crow discrimination and at the hands of police who were a lot more ill-tempered than the officer I tangled with.

Sometimes anger can be a handy conduit for working out our frustration and angst. When the psalmist said, "Be angry, and do not sin" (Psalm 4:4 ESV), I believe he was giving us permission to embrace that anger and tension, but he also warned that we should not allow it to rule. The question is, *What will we do with it?*

KING'S ANGRIEST MOMENT

Dr. King, it seemed, also carried a low-temperature but constant rage within. He endured a lot: death threats, bomb blasts, a stabbing, incarceration. But most of all he endured the strain of knowing his dignity and humanity mattered, even when society and its laws said they didn't. He bore the prophet's burden of knowing it was his responsibility to demand a better reality for his people, a better way for all of America. Yet, America—especially the America of Alabama and Georgia and Mississippi—was not ready to listen. This had to be maddening.

In a 1964 interview King recalled a particularly painful incident from his youth that became a defining moment. At the age of fourteen he traveled with his teacher, Mrs. Sarah Bradley, from Atlanta to Dublin, Georgia, to participate in a speech contest sponsored by the Elks Club. The young King won the competition (go figure) with an address titled "The Negro and the Constitution." After the event King and his teacher boarded a late-night bus back to Atlanta. As they settled into their seats, they were euphoric but tired from the night's proceedings. During a brief stop in a small town along the way, a handful of white passengers boarded the bus. The white bus drive shot a look at King and Mrs. Bradley and commanded them to surrender their seats to the whites. When King and Mrs. Bradley hesitated, the driver spewed profanities at them, calling them "black sons of bitches," and made it clear that he was in no mood for insubordinate Negroes. Feeling stubbornly indignant, King stayed planted in his seat until Mrs. Bradley finally convinced him to move, explaining that they had to obey the law. The student and his teacher stood in the aisle for the remaining ninety miles to Atlanta. King later told an interviewer that he would never forget that event. It was, he said, the angriest he had ever been in his life.

King shared this story after repeated stays in jail, after harassment from the FBI, after having all manner of indignities hurled at him from both segregationist and moderate white critics, and traditionalist and militant black leaders. He was truly hard-pressed from all sides. Yet, an episode from his childhood remained most trenchant in his memory.

"It was the angriest I have ever been in my life."

"Great leaders often have a strong capacity to experience anger," said Columbia Business School professor Hitendra Wadhwa in an *Inc.* magazine article about King's leadership. "It wakes them up and makes them pay attention to what is wrong in their environment, or in themselves. Without anger, they would not have the awareness or the drive to fix what is wrong."

According to King's close friend and supporter, the renowned entertainer Harry Belafonte, "Martin always felt that anger was a very important commodity, a necessary part of the black movement in this country."

And how could it not be?

One of King's gifts as a leader was the ability to see more clearly than most the systemic roots, both spiritual and social, that created the dilemma of racial unrest in the United States. At the zenith of his career, in 1964, he keenly observed that the "frustration" and "desperation" of "the Negro today" was the cumulative effect of prolonged poverty and systematic injustices in housing and public education. He described the black community as being "trapped" in a "socioeconomic vise" and isolated by an "oppressive and constricting prejudice."

But he not only addressed the issues critically. By virtue of his station in life, he experienced them personally. So besides providing sociological analysis, Dr. King likely was also preaching to himself when he added that a righteous man has no choice but to resist such an unrighteous system as Jim Crow. "If he does not have the courage to resist nonviolently," said King, "then he runs the risk of a violent emotional explosion."

In the most crucial moments, King's analytical side allowed him to separate emotion from the problem itself in his quest to interpret conditions for a watching nation. Yet it's clear that he was not a man detached from his feelings.

Unfortunately, King is known more today as a poetic patron saint of racial harmony than a provocative prophet of social justice, someone who by the end of his life had managed to get on just about everyone's last nerve. This surely is one reason why the scholar Cornel West has implored his audiences to resist the "Santa Claus-ification of Martin Luther King." And why historian Tim Tyson lamented, "We have transformed King into a kind of innocuous black Santa Claus, genial and vacant, a benign vessel that can be filled with whatever generic good wishes the occasion dictates."

King, I believe, operated out of a Christian ethic of love that channeled his anger and hurt into a redemptive force for change. He called it "creative nonviolence." And nowhere are the mechanisms of this principled indignation more evident than in the fiery missive he would pen from his Birmingham jail cell.

DUNGEONS AND DARKNESS

Solitary confinement seemed a cruel and unreasonable judgment for peaceably defying an impromptu injunction forbidding public demonstrations. But, then again, nothing was remotely reasonable about this intensifying battle for human rights taking place across the South. Anyone surveying the events happening in Birmingham in the spring of 1963 should've been able to see that.

King sat alone in his dirty, mostly windowless quarters of the city jail. The rusty commode proffered no attached seat, and the tiny bunk, composed of little more than metal slats, sneered in the face of any occupant seriously desirous of unhindered rest. Save for the dim light from a small opening high above, his days were enveloped by gloom. He later said a person will never know the meaning of "utter darkness" until they have spent time in a "dungeon" like the narrow cell he occupied.

For more than twenty-four hours, King was allowed no phone calls and no contact with visitors, not even his lawyers. Though he was treated coldly by the guards, who regarded King as an uppity troublemaker (not to mention other venomous words), there were no acts of physical brutality. Still, he remembered that first day in the Birmingham cell as "the longest, most frustrating and bewildering hours" he had ever lived.

There's never a convenient time to go to jail, but this period was particularly challenging for King, whose wife, Coretta, had just given birth to the couple's fourth child. Already guilt-ridden from being away from his family, and now cut off from contact with the outside world, all he could do was "think long thoughts and pray long prayers."

King was especially concerned that he might fail the thousands who had put their trust in his leadership. He was behind bars at a time when the Birmingham campaign and its so-called Project Confrontation were hobbling and in danger of petering out like the mess that had occurred in Albany. The civil rights leader made a calculated bet that his imprisonment would provide the spark needed to light a wildfire beneath the Birmingham movement, but it could just as easily have become another Albany. What's more, many in the movement worried that King's imprisonment would hinder the fundraising infrastructure needed to secure bail money for the hundreds of youth and young adults who had also gone to jail for marching in the streets. Without the face of the movement on the outside to raise money, the SCLC coffers were running frighteningly dry.

RECLAIMING THE MOMENT

On the Saturday before Easter, the second day of King's stay in solitary confinement, an unidentified jailer slipped him a copy of that morning's edition of the *Birmingham News*, perhaps knowing the Atlanta preacher's blood pressure would rise when he saw the guest editorial on page 2 of the paper. Despite the dim light in King's cell, the headline jumped off the page like the opening credits of a Cecil B. DeMille movie: "WHITE CLERGYMEN URGE LOCAL NEGROES TO WITHDRAW FROM DEMONSTRATIONS."

King pored over the statement from the eight white ministers, his pulse quickening with each line of text. Though the statement did not mention King or the SCLC by name, the insinuation was as loud as a church organ. King homed in on what must have felt to him like a paternalistic censure of the campaign's efforts. He particularly locked in on the suggestion that SCLC leaders were "extremists" and "lawbreakers."

Indulging one's historical imagination and connecting the psychological dots, it's probably safe to surmise King's ego was tweaked. His immediate reaction was likely one of incredulity, followed closely by a sense of betrayal (these were, after all, *moderate* clergymen) and then vexation. It's possible that the sight of the clergymen's statement along with the other stressors in King's mind at that moment combined to create a perfect storm.

"I suspect King was furious," says University of Hartford historian Warren Goldstein. "Things probably looked grim from that jail cell. The movement was faltering again, and it looked like the eight clergymen's interpretation of the situation would win the day and they would dance on his grave."

As he fumed over the ministers' audacity of nope, it's possible that he flashed back and pondered a particularly infuriating moment he experienced in December 1955, during the early stages of the Montgomery bus boycott. As he attempted to reach a resolution with Montgomery's white authorities, it became resoundingly evident that the city's white leaders were unprepared to relinquish their segregated privilege and negotiate in good faith. Instead, they attempted to divide the Negro coalition by portraying King as the main stumbling block to an agreement. Had his colleague Ralph Abernathy not come to his defense, it's possible that the white leaders would have succeeded. Unity in the King-led Montgomery Improvement Association was preserved, but the preacher was incensed. Still mastering the ways of the nonviolent dissenter, he even lost his composure during the meetings. He later recalled that he went home heavy-hearted, weighed down by guilt and regret that he had allowed himself to become angry. He knew even then that the only way to manage a crisis was to maintain control of his emotions, to endure the cruelty of his adversary without returning it in kind. He kept repeating to himself that no matter the situation, he had to remain calm and reject bitterness.

Repeating that mantra no doubt moved King closer to his Christo-Gandhian ideal. Seven years later he had learned to exercise more control over his emotions. Like a mystical Baptist Jedi, he was operating at another level. Rather than allow his anger to congeal into bitterness, he would now use it to reclaim the moment and reframe the Birmingham narrative. He said he became so "upset" and "righteously indignant" that he decided to respond to the letter. But even then, what appeared to be a spontaneous decision was actually part of a larger plan.

THE JAILHOUSE MANIFESTO

Martin Luther King Jr.

NOWADAYS WHEN PASTORS OR CHRISTIAN LEADERS want to vent or share some provocative statement of spiritual consequence, they can simply go to their blogs, Twitter accounts or Facebook pages, where there's usually a captive audience of rapt followers—fans and detractors alike. Many of our most popular evangelical pastors today, in fact, are regularly making news in the so-called Twitterverse by calling out a colleague or offering some offhandedly snide remark. One famous pastor more or less branded a well-known ministerial rival a heretic with a cryptically lucid "farewell." Another big-name minister cynically dismissed the genuineness of a national politician's Christian faith with a 140-character broadside. The social-media missives of today's Christian leaders are often more snarky than prophetic, but they can certainly be useful devices for stoking a like-minded community or tweaking an opponent.

Martin Luther famously used the Wittenberg door as his billboard. Martin Luther King Jr. used pulpits and podiums as his primary platform. But from his lonely cell in the Birmingham City Jail, the agitated preacher prepared to switch his approach.

Beginning in Montgomery, King had identified the press as a crucial partner in his protest efforts and an important key to the effectiveness of his nonviolent methodology. In the latter stages of the Birmingham demonstrations, television would become increasingly important. But as he sat in jail, stewing on the statement from the eight white ministers, he recognized an opportunity to translate the ethical philosophy and moral narrative of the movement into a provocative spiritual treatise that could double as a press release.

CREATIVE (NONVIOLENCE) WRITING

King and his SCLC chief of staff, Rev. Wyatt Tee Walker, had envisioned the Birmingham campaign from the start as a major media spectacle. "My theory was that if we mounted a strong nonviolent movement, the opposition would surely do something to attract the media, and in turn induce national sympathy and attention to the everyday segregated circumstance of a black person living in the Deep South," Walker later explained. But while the physical demonstrations faltered, another expression of resistance was taking shape in King's mind. The concept of an official letter, or epistle, for the civil rights movement actually had been discussed many times among the SCLC leaders. What had been missing was the right raison d'être. Now, however, King saw an opportunity in Birmingham, with the eight white ministers offering themselves up as the perfect foils for his message of Thoreauvian civil disobedience, Gandhian nonviolence and Christian reconciliation.

Compelled by the white ministers, but also by the numerous condemnations of the movement in the local and national media, King grabbed a pen and began to write feverishly in the margins of the *Birmingham News*—up, down and around—until all the blank spaces were filled with his frenzied scrawls.

Here, one might imagine him in the role of the mad scientist or manic genius, a gifted intellect driven by some otherworldly vision or single-minded goal. At least that's the impression I received when I spoke to Martin Luther King Jr.'s lawyer Clarence Jones, who became the intermediary between King the inmate and the SCLC staffers charged with the monumental task of deciphering King's voluminous scribbles and typing them into a readable form.

Jones, a Los Angeles–based attorney, had first met King in February 1960, when the civil rights leader recruited him to help fight a trumped-up tax evasion charge that had been leveled against him by the state of Alabama. King had desired to add the young Negro lawyer to his staff after hearing of his brilliance from a mutual friend. Jones, twenty-nine years old and eager to build his career in entertainment law, initially resisted King's overtures. He reconsidered, however, after pressure from his wife, a wealthy white publishing heiress. Jones helped successfully defend King in the Alabama case and eventually moved to New York to accept a larger role as general counsel for the SCLC. Over time, he would become one of King's most trusted advisers and, along with Stanley Levison, helped shape the political elements of King's speeches.

NO TIME TO WAIT

Coretta King, back home in Atlanta, had not heard from her husband in two days. Worried that he was being mistreated, she used a bit of her clout as the First Lady of the nation's most prominent civil rights leader and phoned the White House for help. By the afternoon of Easter Sunday, King was removed from solitary confinement and permitted to call home. He also was allowed visits from his lawyers.

Appearing at the jail the next day, Clarence Jones wanted to update King on the serious problems facing the movement. Public opinion about the Birmingham campaign's importance was still lagging, and Bull Connor had effectively brought the demonstrations to a halt. "The movement was under siege from Connor as well as the fact that we had hundreds of people who had followed Dr. King in the demonstrations who were locked up in jail," Jones told me. "We didn't have sufficient funds to bail them out, and their families were beginning to exert great pressure on Wyatt Walker and everyone else associated with Martin because we needed to get those protesters out of jail." Jones needed King to give him a list of people he could contact to raise the money, but it was as if King wasn't there. Instead, the civil rights leader was consumed with going over the hodgepodge of paragraphs, biblical phrases and quotations he had written on the edges of the *Birmingham News*, drawing arrows and lines and circles to connect the disparate pieces of text. "He listened to me," recalls Jones, "but he was distracted."

"Look at this," King finally said, holding up the newspaper.

"What are you talking about?" Jones said, becoming increasingly impatient with his client. In addition to the bail issue, there was information from the Kennedy administration and various other grievances that Walker and the SCLC team were grappling with in King's absence. Jones needed King to understand how dire the situation was. But the preacher pointed to the op-ed by the eight white clergymen. "It said, in effect, that we wouldn't have any problems in Birmingham if this outsider Negro preacher would just get out of town." Jones remembers King's visible frustration. "These were good, moderate, religious white people. They said to wait, but Martin was not interested in waiting."

"I'm writing a letter," King revealed, adding that he needed more paper. Jones quietly slid him some sheets from his legal pad. King then handed him the marked-up *Birmingham News* and other scraps of paper filled with his scribbles. "Clarence," he whispered, "you've got to take this out the door and give it to Dora; she can read my writing. You need to take this to her and have her type it." (Dora McDonald was King's personal secretary, but in fact the first drafts of the letter were ultimately transcribed by Wyatt Walker and typed by his twenty-one-year-old secretary, Willie Pearl Mackey.)

Jones, dressed in his best lawyer attire to deflect any risk of rough treatment from the jailers, slipped the paper inside his suit jacket and smuggled it out of the jail, thankful that the guards didn't pat him down. Over the next few days of King's eight-day imprisonment, Jones sneaked in more paper and then faithfully delivered the subsequent notes to the SCLC staff at the Gaston Motel. "Quite frankly, it wasn't until a week later that I paid attention to what he had written, because I had too many other things to do," Jones told me. Among his urgent business was a last-minute trip back to New York to meet with potential donors. "Harry Belafonte had called and said, 'Clarence, how soon can you get to New York?' He had arranged for us to meet with one of Nelson Rockefeller's people." So, after a final jailhouse visit with King, Jones took the last flight out of Birmingham. It would prove to be a propitious appointment, as Jones and Belafonte were able to secure the funds needed for bail money.

GETTING THE WORD OUT

Holed up at the Gaston Motel, Wyatt Walker was ecstatic to receive the piecemeal installments of King's burgeoning manifesto. "His cup has really run over with those white preachers!" Walker declared. Up until then, Walker had been disappointed by his boss's inordinate patience with the obstinacy of the white community. Finally, King was putting words to the ire and frustration that many in the movement had been harboring. Walker knew right away this would be the document that they had long discussed—and written from a jail cell, nonetheless, just like Paul's prison epistles. He decided early on that King's "chicken-scratched" essay would have far-reaching significance for the movement.

Later on, Jones realized, too, just how profound those miscellaneous scraps of paper were.

When I finally read Dr. King's "Letter," more than anyone else, I said, "Oh, my God! I can't believe this," because I had seen the circumstances under which he created it. He didn't have a single book to refer to. He didn't have anything in that cell with him. I mean, he was a Ph.D. in theology, so I'm not surprised by his encyclopedic knowledge of the Bible. But when you read that letter, it's full of references from philosophy and great writers. He's quoting poetry; he's quoting learned political theorists; he's talking about St. Augustine and St. Thomas Aquinas. It's powerful.

Almost fifty years later, Jones, now a scholar-in-residence at Stanford University, was still astonished by his friend's genius. "Listen," he told me,

when I drafted speeches for Dr. King on a particular matter and you'd come into a room where I'd be working, you'd see about twenty-five open books spread around my desk. But King had a photographic mind. I thought to myself after reading the letter that this was incredible, that he could sit and write something so cogent, so erudite, so persuasive on scraps of paper. It is still to me one of the greatest pieces of political advocacy and religious writing that I have ever read.

REFRAMING THE QUESTION

Ella Josephine Baker, the behind-the-scenes civil rights heroine whose career in fighting for social justice for African Americans spanned five decades beginning in the 1930s, made a statement that has become vital in explaining the phenomenon that is Martin Luther King Jr. In talking about King's emergence and rise as the preeminent civil rights champion of the modern era, she famously said, "It was the movement that made Martin rather than Martin making the movement." And there's certainly truth to that statement. Each generation stands on the shoulders of the earlier ones, and King did not invent the role of the black civil rights leader. His work clearly benefited from a foundation laid by the many other brave men and women who struggled for social justice before him—such as Frederick Douglass, Booker T. Washington, and W. E. B. Du Bois—but also activists who were, to varying degrees, contemporaries of King such as Baker or the Rev. Vernon Johns, who pastored Dexter Avenue Baptist Church in Montgomery before King. Still, it also could be argued that the movement King led was one transformed by the unique mix of ideas and gifts that he alone brought to the picture. As historian and preaching scholar Richard Lischer has said:

> The Civil Rights Movement did not "make" King any more than the Civil War "made" Lincoln. Admittedly, like Lincoln, King was summoned by events he did not initiate and exposed to conditions he did not create, but his response was so powerful an interpretation of events that it reshaped the conditions in which they originated. His answer was so true that it reframed the question.

It's wise to avoid hagiography; we need to place a leader like King in his proper context. That means recognizing his flaws, but also acknowledging the inestimable contributions of countless other less-celebrated but equally courageous civil rights warriors and foot soldiers whose efforts propelled the movement. King obviously couldn't do it alone. Crucial leadership also came from prominent King contemporaries' such as Fred Shuttlesworth, CORE founder James Farmer, National Council of Negro Women president Dorothy Height, SNCC leader John Lewis, labor movement organizer A. Philip Randolph, NAACP chief Roy Wilkins, and National Urban League president Whitney Young. That King should emerge as the most prominent voice from among the movement heavyweights was not only a result of his considerable gifts (each member brought their own unique talents and constituencies) but of internal politics and the movement's need to project a unified vision to the nation.

As his work grew from local protests into a national phenomenon, "Martin Luther King Jr." became not simply a man but also a collective idea—a symbol. This, no doubt, was partly to blame for the chronic exhaustion he would suffer later in his career. As the movement expanded, King became a man possessed of an unstoppable vision but with little control over the events driving it. "I need your help," King often said to prospective collaborators. "I have no idea where this movement is going." His "Letter from Birmingham Jail," however, would exemplify one of those singular moments when the genius of King both drew on and transcended the strength of the larger movement.

9

"My Dear Fellow Clergymen"

During the night Paul had a vision of a
man of Macedonia standing and begging him,
"Come over to Macedonia and help us."
Acts 16:9 NIV

Martin Luther King Jr.

Dated April 16, 1963, Dr. King's letter from the Birmingham City Jail was ostensibly addressed to the eight white clergymen who had deemed him an "outsider" and called his movement's presence in Birmingham "unwise" and "untimely." King explains that, as a rule, he avoids responding directly to the multitude of criticisms leveled against him. But because he senses these brothers are "men of genuine goodwill" and that their "criticisms are sincerely set forth," he endeavors to answer them in "patient and reasonable terms."

He begins, "My Dear Fellow Clergymen." But it becomes evident fairly quickly that he isn't just aiming his missive at clerics Harmon, Hardin, Carpenter, Durick, Grafman, Murray, Ramage and Stallings. No, for him the Birmingham Eight are essentially surrogates for the larger watching world. King is *also* going after Birmingham's new mayor, Albert Boutwell, Commissioner Bull Connor, his African American critics, President John F. Kennedy, Attorney General Robert F. Kennedy, Billy Graham and every other American, white or black, who felt Negroes should slow their proverbial roll or who doubted the Judeo-Christian foundations of civil disobedience and nonviolent resistance.

"Letter from Birmingham Jail" marks a synthesis of concepts and philosophies King had been working out for years in speeches, articles and even in his seminary and postgraduate work. It represents, in the opinion of one historian, "a culmination of all of King's ideas, theology, experiences, and civil rights tactics." His approach is at once redemptive *and* subversive. There is, in effect, a method to his meekness. Notes Thoreau scholar Wesley T. Mott, "King's conciliatory tone—while apparently conceding ground in its humility—is intended to reveal the inhumanity of the clergymen's position and to hold it up to the scorn of those of us who are reading over their shoulders."

KING WITHOUT BORDERS

King works hard to establish a tone of cordial discourse, but through each sentence we can feel his fierce indignation teeming below the surface. When the letter finally found its way to the Birmingham Eight, they no doubt felt it too.

King likens himself to the apostle Paul, who traveled throughout Greece and Asia Minor preaching and launching churches (and who also, coincidentally, spent a lot of time writing letters to the church from behind bars). King cites the "Macedonian call," in which a man appears to Paul in a dream, asking him to "come over to Macedonia and help us" (Acts 16:9). Like King, Paul was persecuted, arrested and ultimately executed for preaching an unpopular message. King connects his own situation to Paul's sufferings and thus ascribes a level of biblical legitimacy to his ministry of social justice. He justifies his presence in Birmingham by appealing to "the interrelatedness of all communities and states" and declaring that his quest for human rights transcends jurisdiction. He could not "sit idly by in Atlanta" while hell was breaking loose in Birmingham. Injustice anywhere threatens justice everywhere, he says.

To the criticism that the Birmingham demonstrations were ill-timed, King counters that those in privileged positions cannot be depended on to yield their power voluntarily—they must be compelled to do right. He alludes to the words of Frederick Douglass, who declared in a famous 1857 speech, "Power concedes nothing without a demand." In addition, King cites theologian Reinhold Niebuhr, another one of his intellectual heroes, to drive home the argument that change is more difficult for groups than for individuals.

King shoots down the notion that his movement's campaign is "untimely" by contending that any move against the status quo will be viewed as poorly timed by those who are beneficiaries of the current system. It's another story, however, for those living under its oppression.

What comes next are some of the letter's most poignant and sermonic lines, as King riffs on the absurdity of the word *wait* for the African American. It might be simple for people who have not experienced "the stinging darts of segregation" to say "wait," but those who have witnessed lynchings and police brutality and brutal poverty against the backdrop of immense American wealth . . . You're going to tell them to *wait?* King wades deeper into autobiographical waters by referencing the pain of a Negro parent having to tell his small child that she's not allowed to go to a public amusement park because of her race. How could they expect a people who are "harried by day and haunted by night" by racism to accept waiting?

Next, King takes on the central question raised by the Birmingham Eight: How could he be so selective about law and order, encouraging Negroes to violate some laws while conversely urging whites to abide by such judicial rulings as *Brown v. Board of Education*? King points to the concept of "eternal law" and "natural law" as expressed in the thought of Augustine and Thomas Aquinas. A humanly devised law is "just" if it's consistent with the divinely established call to uplift and improve humanity. Those types of laws should be obeyed. But a person has a moral duty to *disobey* unjust laws, such as the Jim Crow laws that rule the Deep South. Those laws are unjust because they distort human character and worth, giving "the segregator a false sense of superiority and the segregated a false sense of inferiority."

King also wants his readers to acknowledge that a just law may be *unjustly* applied—that is, a law that is inherently good or neutral can be twisted into something harmful. Requiring a municipal permit for a parade, for instance, is not wrong. But it can become unjust when used to impose segregation and deny some citizens their right to peaceful assembly and protest.

Finally, in the letter's longest and perhaps most condemning section, King registers his deep frustration with "the white moderate," who supposedly agrees with the goal of integration and equal rights but objects to the nonviolent confrontational approach of his movement. Change can only come, King believes, by exposing the dysfunction already embedded in a society. In a calculated moment of hyperbolic exasperation, he essentially groups the halfhearted moderate, presumably including the Birmingham Eight, in the same boat with white supremacists such as "the Ku Klux Klanner" or "the White Citizen's Counciler."

The white clergymen described the Birmingham protesters as "extremists." Perhaps wanting them to understand the patronizing and simplistic nature of their accusation, King shares a bit of his own struggle of being caught in the midst of a very fluid and dynamic tension in the black community. In a fascinating sequence of profound introspection, King initially resists the "extremist" characterization. Instead, he places himself on the map as a moderate caught between middle-class Negroes who have settled into complacency and bowed to segregation and the Black Muslims who view white people as "the devil." These two are your "extremists," King insists. To call black people who believe in peaceful protest and equality among the races extreme is ludicrous. King suggests that protests against segregation may actually have a therapeutic benefit. Whites should not view them as a disruption to the status quo but as a positive alternative to chaos and violence. "Oppressed people cannot remain oppressed forever," King writes. "The yearning for freedom eventually manifests itself." American Negroes had been "caught up by the *Zeitgeist*" of the times and "with his black brothers of Africa and his brown and yellow brothers of Asia, South America and the Caribbean" were "moving with a sense of great urgency toward the promised land of racial justice." Therefore, King beseeches his readers to understand that these demands for freedom are not the acts of extremists but the natural impulse of a people who have been denied their humanity.

However, after reflecting on the extremist tag a bit more, King doubles back. "Was not Jesus an extremist?" he asks. What about the prophet Amos? The apostle Paul? The Protestant Reformer Martin Luther? Declaration of Independence architect Thomas Jefferson? The great emancipator Abe Lincoln? What about Jesus himself? Weren't all of these leaders considered extremists in their day? On second thought, King seems to say, maybe the world needs a few more "creative extremists."

Historian Stewart Burns sees in this episode an instance of King perhaps wrestling with himself over where he resided on the spectrum and where he actually belonged. On the matter of "extremists," Burns suggests the preacher was not just speaking to the clergymen and America but to himself as well:

> In a semiconscious way he may have been addressing his own moderate, cautious, and passive side. He could identify with the middle-class white clergy; perhaps this was why he challenged them so artfully. He had always leaned toward caution and often appeared passive. . . . He had refused to join the freedom rides even after egging on the riders. He had wiggled and wavered in Albany, further infuriating his SNCC allies. He had reluctantly approved the Birmingham campaign only when Shuttlesworth's pleading could not be rebuffed. In his upbringing and temperament he was as much a moderate as the bishops and rabbi he was upbraiding. Putting aside his own comfortable moderate demeanor, he had to decide for himself, *What kind of extremist shall I be?*

In other words—and this certainly isn't any kind of breaking news—the "Letter from Birmingham Jail" and the Birmingham campaign in general perhaps not only represented the maturation of King's message but also his acceptance of the role of a civil rights radical.

But even as he's dispensing some of his letter's harshest rhetoric, King slows down to offer a salute to a number of Southern whites who, unlike too many of their moderate kin, had put their necks on the line to battle segregation and support the movement.

The tributes, though, are short-lived, as King quickly launches back into a blistering indictment of the white church in America and its refusal to get behind the freedom movement, its proclivity to act "more cautious than courageous" and its tendency to remain "silent behind the anesthetizing security of stained-glass windows." Though he praises one of the Birmingham Eight by name (Rev. Earl Stallings, who had admirably refused to expel a group of black worshipers from his church on the previous Easter Sunday despite the protestations of some of his congregants), overall King is distraught that the majority of white ministers urged their people to comply with unjust segregation laws. He's dismayed by their "un-Biblical" separation of the sacred and the secular. For King, of course, the call of the gospel requires that attention be paid to both soul and body. The gospel of individual salvation is not complete; it must be supplemented by the social gospel, lest the whole enterprise become spiritually dead. King warns that unless the church recaptures the boldness and sacrificial spirit of the early Christians, it was in danger of becoming socially irrelevant.

And were these pastors actually giving props to the efforts of the Birmingham police for "keeping order" and "preventing violence"? The same police that had routinely conspired with the KKK and that soon would unleash German shepherds on innocent marchers? King knew that Bull Connor's use of restraint was calculated and fleeting. Connor's use of the moral means of nonviolence toward the immoral end of racial segregation was wrong, said King, who invoked T. S. Eliot to drive his point home, writing, "The last temptation is the greatest treason: To do the right deed for the wrong reason." Rather than commending a corrupt police force, shouldn't those pastors be praising the bravery and self-control of the protesters? He adds that someday the South will recognize its true heroes. He cites college student James Meredith, who had courageously integrated the University of Mississippi, and the countless other "disinherited children of God" as being representative of those true heroes. But the Birmingham police? *C'mon now*, King seems to implore. But despite his incredulity, he manages to maintain a civil, though unyielding, tone to the end.

He wraps up his letter on a gracious note, begging pardon for his long-windedness. He hopes that one day he may be able to meet the clergymen in person, "not as . . . a civil rights leader" but as "a Christian brother." With all the hard stuff out of the way, one gets the feeling that King really is sincere in this wish.

Sadly, King and the Birmingham Eight would never meet face to face. And in some cases King's strong words would prove utterly devastating to the clergymen's post–"Letter from Birmingham Jail" lives. But in the intersections of history, faith and social justice, these nine men *have* met and are in constant communication.

FROM MONOLOGUE TO DIALOGUE

I like to imagine the "Letter from Birmingham Jail" as more than just a one-sided beatdown of the eight white ministers. I like to envision it as a running dialogue between Dr. King and those Birmingham Eight. In the annals of history, it's a conversation that we're not only privileged to overhear but that we're obliged to act on in the present as a result of our hearing it. Piecing together paraphrased excerpts from the two clashing statements, here's what a portion of the conversation might sound like:

> *Birmingham Eight:* Dr. King, we appreciate what you were able to accomplish in Montgomery when you lived there, but this is Birmingham. Why are you bringing a group of outsiders to our city? We believe our local white and Negro leadership should work together to solve our city's problems.
>
> *King:* Well, as president of the Southern Christian Leadership Conference, I received an invitation from our Alabama affiliate. But even more important, I came to Birmingham because injustice is here.
>
> *Birmingham Eight:* Okay, we understand the impatience of people who feel their hopes are slow in coming. But we are convinced that these demonstrations are happening at the wrong time and will only sabotage the slow but sure steps we're taking toward progress. Now is not the right time.
>
> *King:* Look, brothers, I have yet to engage in a campaign that was "well timed" for those who are not the targets of oppression. I've been hearing "Wait!" for too many years. It rings in the ear of every Negro like a radio jingle. But it almost always means

"Never." And, like William Gladstone said, justice too long
delayed is justice denied.

Birmingham Eight: We simply cannot support protest methods like
sit-ins and marches that lead to hatred and violence, no matter
how "peaceful" those methods are from your perspective. We
think open and honest negotiation is a better way.

King: You're absolutely correct to call for honest negotiation, but it
takes two to tango. Both sides have to be willing to talk. Our
nonviolent direct action is designed to create the kind of crisis that
will foster tension in a community that has consistently refused to
negotiate. Our protests will force them to the table. That's our
strategy—to create a situation so intense that it will inevitably
open the door to negotiation. I understand your anxiety. But the
truth is, our beloved Southland has been bogged down too long in
a tragic effort to live in monologue rather than dialogue.

Birmingham Eight: Dr. King, at the end of the day, this is all about
keeping the law. We believe a society functions best when it
adheres to a system of law and order. When the rights of our
Negro citizens are consistently denied, this should be pressed in
the courts and in negotiations among local leaders—not in the
streets. Whether you're white or black, you must obey the law.
Otherwise, we'll be creating a recipe for anarchy.

King: You're bothered by our readiness to break laws. I get it. This
is certainly a legitimate concern. After all, we've urged white
people to abide by the *Brown v. the Board of Education* decision.
So, it's fair to ask, How can you advocate breaking some laws
and obeying others? Well, the answer lies in the fact that there
are two types of laws: just and unjust. A person has a duty to
obey just laws; however, he also has a moral obligation not to
obey unjust laws. I agree with St. Augustine on this one: "an
unjust law is no law at all."

Unfortunately, King and his eight fellow clergymen did not experience this kind of vigorous back-and-forth personally. Their relationship never left the realm of rhetoric and symbol. There would

be no opportunity for one-on-one reconciliation. "Perhaps in a less emotional time, in a calm setting, these ministers would have met face-to-face and discussed their differences," historian Jonathan Bass speculates, "but this was Birmingham, 1963."

READING THEIR MAIL

When the eight ministers to whom "Letter from Birmingham Jail" was addressed finally saw it weeks later, most of them believed it was "cruel and unfair," writes Bass. Their individual responses represented "a mixed bag" that revealed shifting combinations of anger, sadness and acceptance.

- Earl Stallings, the Baptist minister, the only minister who had been mentioned (favorably) by name, believed King had made a "clear presentation" of what he perceived the situation to be, but also felt that King misunderstood the depth of his commitment to racial inclusivity.

- Edward Ramage, the Presbyterian pastor, compared reading the letter for the first time to receiving an epistle from the apostle Paul; however, Ramage later expressed regret that it might be the only thing his ministry would be remembered for.

- Paul Hardin, the Methodist bishop, believed King was correct on most of his points. "White ministers should have taken a more active role during the crisis," Hardin said. Still, he lamented that King's letter did not truly capture "the personal convictions" of the Birmingham Eight.

- George Murray, the Episcopalian bishop, objected to King's rhetorical stunt of quoting Scripture against the group and setting them up as "straw men." He also was confused that the civil rights leader would address them when their statement had been to Birmingham's *local* black leaders. To his mind, King had "misconstrued" their intentions.

- Nolan Harmon, the other Methodist bishop, felt betrayed by the letter and believed King should have sent it to them first before releasing it to the media as a "propaganda" tool. He insisted that integration could only come through "gradualism" and "law and order."

- Charles Carpenter, another Episcopalian bishop, saw the letter as "careless criticism" and, according to Bass, viewed any civil disobedience as "a terrible transgression against genteel southern society."

- Rabbi Milton Grafman described the letter as "a beautiful yet vicious" piece of writing. He was irate that King would cast the eight leaders forever as "bigots" in the minds of the public. He was offended by the idea of outsiders projecting their liberal prejudices on Southerners. When a delegation of Northern rabbis descended on Birmingham to show their support for African Americans during the 1963 demonstrations, Grafman regarded them as misguided grandstanders who had no sense of the real issues facing the people of Birmingham.

- Joseph Durick saw the letter as both an arrow and a mirror. Out of all the clergymen, Durick's reaction was probably the most positive, and he appeared to be the leader most transformed by the letter's message. The Catholic bishop said he understood King's need to use them as a foil. And though he was disappointed that they were never able to have personal interaction around the race issue, he acknowledged that the letter had a powerful effect on his thinking, even motivating him to fight harder for racial justice. Inspired by King's letter, Durick would go on to lead his Birmingham diocese toward genuine integration.

As is the case with all of us, each of the Birmingham Eight experienced the letter differently based on his individual journey and perspective. Their subsequent defiance, denial or embrace of

King's message says as much about the human aspect of "Letter from Birmingham Jail" as it does about the ethical dimension. Though it was conceived as a device for promoting the civil rights movement's agenda, the letter became much more—for King, for the eight clergymen and for all of us who would eventually read it.

KING'S SECRET

It's fair to criticize King's calculated use of the Birmingham Eight's statement and the media to get his movement's message across, but it also should be noted that King was not operating in a historical vacuum when he wrote "Letter from Birmingham Jail." He had seen and understood the stubbornness of white Southern leaders; he had come face-to-face with the viciousness of the segregationist machine. He knew that relying on an unjust system of law would never lead to true justice. And so the notion that King recklessly appropriated the eight ministers as "straw men" is shortsighted. King's mention of Stallings's name showed that the preacher recognized the humanity of the eight ministers. But King was also desperate to access the divine power of words and ideas—as opposed to fear and violence—to change a nation. He was a man on a single-minded mission, and there's no question that the Birmingham Eight's well-intentioned op-ed aided him in achieving his goal.

Despite moments of self-doubt, King operated in a confidence that the movement he was called to lead would ultimately be successful because, as he wrote to the clergymen, "the sacred heritage of our nation and the eternal will of God are embodied in our echoing demands." King put the onus on American democracy. He knew that if the idea of America was true, then its veracity would be judged by the fate of its most marginalized people. He believed in God, and this gave him faith to believe in America's lofty ideals of fairness and freedom. He could march and suffer and go to jail knowing that he was working for a divine and righteous cause.

Still, King faced a gargantuan task in Birmingham. He was compelled to address the gauntlet thrown down before him by the white clergymen. But he also was mindful that what he wrote in response could define the course of the whole civil rights movement going forward. What flowed out of his soul, through his pen and onto paper during those dark days in the Birmingham City Jail needed to rise to the occasion.

How did he do it?

First and foremost a man of prayer, King knew that his solitary confinement was only a physical state of being. "God's companionship does not stop at the door of a jail cell," he later wrote about his Birmingham experience. "God had been my cellmate." This probably best explains why "Letter from Birmingham Jail" became such a powerful document. King did not write it alone.

TAKING IT
TO THE STREETS

Martin Luther King Jr.

MICHAEL WESLEY HAS OBSERVED a grit and decency in the attitudes of young people that keeps him hopeful for the future of race relations in this country. He even reserves some optimism for the older generations.

Before he became the senior pastor of Greater Shiloh Baptist Church in Birmingham, Wesley worked as an educator in the city school system—a system he knew well from his days as a student. As an African American he often has found himself right in the middle of the action for many of the public school system's key milestones. In 1968, when school desegregation was finally gaining traction in Birmingham, Wesley was among the first group of black students to integrate the previously all-white Ramsay High School. "At that time, racial tensions were still pretty strong," he remembers. "Some people did not know how to negotiate their differences or act toward each other." So, by and large, students stayed in their own segregated communities. Initially there was "name calling" and occasional "racial slurs" exchanged between students. But slowly, people began reaching across racial lines. "As I participated in the school band and various athletic programs, I was able to build friendships even against the warnings and wishes of some parents and teachers."

Though the laws had changed, Wesley realized there was still an "old guard" that sought to preserve the traditional way of life in Birmingham. But during those natural times when the students were allowed to just be students and not "colored kids" or "white kids," Wesley saw the potential for change, and it gave him hope. "Largely, those four years of high school went along very well," he says.

Wesley says he developed a good balance in his life as a result of those early experiences. "I wasn't in the direct line of a lot of the race stuff, doing the demonstrations and that kind of thing," he explains. "But I saw myself as a beneficiary of the doors of opportunity being cracked open." Those open doors afforded him "a good high school education" as well as degrees from Tennessee State University in Nashville and Samford University in Birmingham. He worked in the school district for twenty-six years, as a teacher and then later a principal. Another milestone was achieved when, in the late 1990s, he became the first African American principal at Woodlawn, "the largest high school in Birmingham." The opportunity was especially meaningful to him because, years earlier, his mother had worked in the school's lunchroom. "She was there during those times when segregation was in its heyday," he says. "I remember riding with my father to pick my mother up from work and he wasn't permitted to drive in the front of the school because we were black; he always had to go to the back." Forty years later, Wesley was running the school. "My mother was still alive at that point," he says, "so it was a privilege for me to honor her during the first graduation that I presided over by sharing her story with the graduates and audience that day."

As an educator Wesley says he was always encouraged by the sight of black kids and white kids building friendships "without all the racial issues" getting in the way.

Back in 1963, however, it was impossible for students in Birmingham—well, at least Negro students—to *not* think about race. Wesley was only nine that year, but he remembers his older sister, Janice, being jailed for several days after her arrest for taking part in the first day of the pivotal children's march. His older brother, Alvin, marched the next day and was on the receiving end of the police dogs and fire hoses. It was a dramatic turning point in the Birmingham campaign that, more or less, saved the entire movement from ruin. But the march almost didn't happen. And if it had been up to Dr. King alone, it almost certainly wouldn't have.

PLAN B FOR PROJECT C

After eight days in the Birmingham jail, Martin Luther King and Ralph Abernathy were released. However, it would be at least another month before King's "Letter from Birmingham Jail" appeared anywhere in the press, and much longer than that before the public would come to recognize it as his great epistle to the church, America and the world. Later, in a much more polished form, it would appear in numerous magazines and ultimately as part of King's 1964 tome, *Why We Can't Wait*. But for the immediate challenges before the Birmingham movement's leaders, they could not rely on the publicity or inspirational rush that the letter would eventually afford.

Meanwhile, a civil rights victory was far from sealed in Birmingham. King's imprisonment had not been the galvanizing force he had hoped. Outside the jail cell, the campaign was still languishing. The media had begun to leave the city, and King became both desperate and mad. "We've got to pick up everything, because the press is leaving," he said. "We've got to *get going*." King realized right away that something radical would need to be done to prevent the effort from joining "Albany, Georgia," in the annals of civil rights flops.

It was at this point that King decided to call in James Bevel, a passionate SCLC field organizer who was a veteran of the Nashville sit-ins. The twenty-six-year-old Bevel initiated what would become the most controversial phase of Project C: the use of children and teenagers. Bevel recalled later, "Up to this point, about five to ten, maybe twelve people would go and demonstrate each day. My position was you can't get the dialogues you need with a few." Bevel knew the demonstrations would need thousands of bodies in the streets to rattle Bull Connor and create the disturbing imagery that the nation needed to see. But how could he get thousands of people onto the streets without creating an economic crisis by asking people to miss work to protest? His solution: recruit high school students. "We started organizing the prom queens of the high schools, the basketball stars, the football stars, to get the influence and power leaders involved. They in turn got all the other students involved. The black community as a whole did not have that kind of cohesion or camaraderie. But the students, they had a community they'd been in since elementary school, so they bonded quite well." It meant they could form a united front and find empowerment through marching together, facing the police together, going to jail together.

King rejected Bevel's plan outright. A. G. Gaston decried "the invasion of our schools" to recruit kids. Another minister was shocked that Bevel wanted to urge students to disobey their parents. Not surprisingly, Fred Shuttlesworth was open to the idea: "Sometimes you have to raise them so they'll be people on their own," he said. But King wasn't buying it.

Finally, Bevel challenged King with a question he knew the Baptist preacher couldn't escape: "How old does a child need to be to accept Christ?" King knew that age didn't make a difference in a person's salvation as long as they were making a "conscious decision." So why, Bevel persisted, should the kids not also be allowed to make a conscious decision about their freedom? King received the point. Though he was still reluctant to put young people at such great risk, he warmed to the idea as he determined that a situation as crazy and irrational as the one in Birmingham would require an equally crazy and irrational response. He also genuinely believed that young people should have their own stake in the fight for freedom. But most of all, he was probably desperate for something that would salvage the campaign. With nerves on edge, he gave Bevel permission to move forward with the plan. The Children's Crusade was on.

MAKING IT PERSONAL

Janice Kelsey (née Wesley) was a sixteen-year-old student at Birmingham's Ullman High School when she got word of the mass meetings at Sixteenth Street Baptist Church. Several of her friends were going, and it was a way to show her support for the faltering movement in her city. Some of her girlfriends also mentioned that the SCLC's leaders were handsome and could sing, so that was a nice incentive to attend as well.

At the meeting she listened to speeches by King, Shuttlesworth and others. "But James Bevel was actually the one that said some things that touched me personally," she remembers. "He talked about the inequities between the white schools and the colored schools, how the football uniforms at our school were discards from white schools." Bevel then pointed out how the white schools had new electric typewriters while the black schools still had manual machines. "That was particularly offensive to me," Janice says. Why, continued Bevel, were black customers at the J. J. Newberry's five-and-dime required to stand and eat their hotdogs and Cokes while white patrons could sit in booths on the main level? "Given examples like that, I became convinced that I was being treated like a second-class citizen," says Janice. "I was aware that segregation existed, but James Bevel made it personal."

Bevel challenged the students to march for their freedom, but he warned them that they would likely be arrested. No matter. Janice and her friends were in—ready to march, ready to go to jail. She says they were emboldened by "the sense that we could do something about this inequity." The students also determined that "we were really the only ones who could do something." They knew that if the adults marched, they could risk going to jail, jeopardizing their jobs and possibly leaving some children without mothers and fathers at home. "So it was up to us," says Janice.

PARTY AT THE PARK

The teenagers, as well as many elementary school students, brought boundless enthusiasm to the Birmingham effort. They signed up for the protests by the hundreds and were promptly trained in the movement's nonviolence methodology. On the morning of May 2— dubbed "D-Day" by Bevel—the deejay on the local Negro radio station announced, "There's gonna be a party at the park." It was coded language that Janice understood. She packed her purse with a toothbrush and other items she thought she'd need for a couple nights away. "I did not seek my mother's permission," she says, adding that she likely suspected something was afoot. Recalls Janice: "She told me, 'I'm sending you to school. Don't you go anywhere and get yourself in trouble, because I don't have any money to get you out of jail.' I said, 'Yes, Ma'am,' and I did go to school—but I knew I wasn't going to stay there. I just didn't share that part with her."

Janice and her friends did go to school, but when the signal was given, "We walked out in droves." Some of the teachers attempted to stop them, remembers Janice, but others quietly turned their backs to write on the blackboard while their pupils vacated the classrooms.

The mass of students walked the short distance from Ullman High School to Sixteenth Street Baptist Church, laughing and singing all the way. "There were kids everywhere," says Janice. "They were outside in Kelly Ingram Park [across from the church], on the church steps, and spilling out from the church sanctuary. There were hundreds upon hundreds of kids—from high school, grade school, and even college." She noticed that there was also a throng of police officers lining the streets.

Bevel and SCLC deputy Andrew Young were organizing the events that day, says Janice. They called the students into the church, where they prayed and sang freedom songs before separating the group into those who would march and those who would remain at the church to create placards or other volunteer work. "They kept reiterating that it was going to be a nonviolent march," recalls Janice. "They said we might be hit or called names, and if we couldn't handle that, we should not go out on the march." The marchers walked out in pairs, singing "We Shall Overcome." But they didn't get far.

"We were maybe a block from the church, heading north to city hall, when the policeman told us that we were in violation of a city ordinance and that we couldn't parade without a permit," says Janice, who remembers it as "quite an intimidating scene." At first, all she could see were the "billy stick in his hand and the pistol on his hip," but then someone started singing "We Are Not Afraid," and it began to resonate throughout the whole group. It gave them the courage needed to keep going. They were loaded by the dozens into "paddy wagons" that Janice says were designed to hold four people at the most. "They shoved us and called us ugly names, but we took it all in stride."

The marchers were instructed not to give the authorities any information about their families, to avoid making their homes a target for bombings or their parents targets for termination at their workplaces. "We just gave them our name and age," says Janice, who was taken to makeshift jail cells at the state fairgrounds because the city and county jails were so crammed with children. More than eight hundred kids were incarcerated that day. It was at least three times the number of adults who had been arrested during the entire month of April.

The next day, not wanting to be outdone by his younger sister, Janice's seventeen-year-old brother Alvin joined the second wave of marchers. However, Alvin's experience would be different. Though nearly a thousand kids were arrested the first day, for the most part there was little physical confrontation from the police. But on day two, with the marchers filling his jail beyond capacity, Bull Connor lost whatever cool he had managed to maintain earlier and commanded his men to get nasty. As even more children and teens marched across Kelly Ingram Park in downtown Birmingham chanting, "We're going to walk for freedom," Connor returned to form.

"I was in jail when they brought the police dogs and fire hoses," says Janice, "but my brother was there, and he got the brunt of it." He described a horrific scene of kids being bitten by the German shepherds and toppled by the high-pressure water cannons. "I had one friend who said she actually had some of her hair sheared off of her head by the water," recalls Janice. "People had bruises on their bodies, and some had their clothes torn by the force of the water. It was bad."

To force the marchers back toward the park, the police began using their billy clubs without restraint. The Rev. A. D. King, Martin's younger brother and the pastor of a church in Birmingham, attempted to lead one group of marchers to city hall but was intercepted by police. A. D. King would be among the sprinkling of adults to be arrested during this "youth" phase of the campaign.

Fred Burnett, a white Birmingham native who is now a professor of religion at the Anderson University School of Theology in Indiana, was an eighteen-year-old student in 1963. As the madness was escalating on May 3, Burnett and two of his friends had just finished watching a movie in downtown Birmingham. Exiting the theater, they were greeted with the inexplicable scene of throngs of blacks, many their age, marching two by two. They were walking and singing songs, yet the police were siccing dogs on them and the firefighters were spraying them with water. Burnett and his friends couldn't quite make sense of what was happening. Were the Negroes trying to take over the city just like Commissioner Connor and Governor Wallace had warned? No, these Negroes appeared to be marching peacefully. Were they just being "happy Negroes," always singing and dancing like Negroes do? No, these marchers appeared to be dignified and focused. Or were they just simple-minded creatures, with "smaller brains than whites," as Burnett and his friends had always been taught? But that didn't make sense either. After all, Burnett wondered, "Who has the smaller brain, the eight-year-old black girl being hosed or the adult white fireman hosing her?" Looking back, Burnett realizes that he and his friends were "confronted by an event of such magnitude" that nothing in his eighteen-year-old, white Southern worldview could credibly explain it. "The 'truth' as I had been given it just didn't fit the event."

Two years later, when Burnett was a student at Anderson University, the college president invited everyone to participate in a "sympathy march," walking from the campus to the local courthouse, to demonstrate support for Martin Luther King Jr.'s Selma-to-Montgomery march that was taking place in Alabama. Most of the students chose to remain on campus, but Burnett marched. He had to. What he had witnessed in Birmingham in May 1963 had changed his perspective forever.

"THIS HAS BECOME EVERYTHING"

Bull Connor had played into the movement's hands. Though the local newspapers buried the story in their interior pages and refused to publish photos of the turmoil, the national media swooped in and transmitted the disturbing images to a shocked America. Suddenly public sentiment began turning in favor of King and his marchers. People from around the country sent money to fund the campaign, and even some members of Birmingham's white community joined the boycott of downtown businesses.

From the White House in Washington, D.C., President Kennedy surveyed the turmoil as well. "This has become everything," he said. Not wanting to upset Southern Democrats, Kennedy had done his best to steer clear of civil rights controversies, but Birmingham was exposing the nation's invisible "Negro problem" for the whole world to see. His brother Robert was also aghast at the situation, especially the involvement of the young people. "An injured, maimed or dead child is a price none of us can afford to pay," said the attorney general. Desperate to defuse the situation, the Kennedys dispatched Assistant Attorney General Burke Marshall to Birmingham to help negotiate a truce.

Still, over the next few days the situation spiraled. With some of the young marchers growing restless and throwing rocks and other debris at policemen, the SCLC leaders had to work harder to keep the protests nonviolent. But with each day, emotions became more frayed. Fred Shuttlesworth, faithfully providing adult leadership in the middle of the chaos, was blasted by a fire-hose torrent so violent that it knocked him down a stairwell at Sixteenth Street Baptist Church and smashed him against a wall. His injuries were so severe that he had to be rushed to the hospital. Hearing that Shuttlesworth had been carried away in an ambulance, Bull Connor said, "I wish they'd carried him away in a hearse."

Meanwhile, King worked hard to calm the fears of the understandably nervous parents of the student protesters. The young people were marching for themselves and for future generations, he told them. King and Andrew Young also met with Burke Marshall and white city leaders in ongoing talks to bring an end to the demonstrations. The white businessmen were eager to end the boycotts and restore order to the downtown area. King was desperate to get Birmingham's courageous children off the streets and out of jail. Finally, King agreed to a deal that had been brokered by Marshall for a suspension of the demonstrations while the two sides continued to talk. President Kennedy was set to make the announcement from the White House, while King would speak from Birmingham. But before it could happen, Fred Shuttlesworth, who had just been released from the hospital, squashed the deal. "We will not end the demonstrations until we have an agreement," he said. In one of the campaign's tensest moments, Shuttlesworth and King went toe-to-toe over the issue.

"We agreed to call it off," King explained. "The merchants said they can't negotiate with the demonstrations going on." Shuttlesworth, however, wasn't hearing it: "Hell, no, Martin," he snapped. "When you came into Birmingham, you didn't ask permission from President Kennedy. Burke Marshall . . . wasn't nowhere around. There was some people here who had confidence in me, because they knew I wasn't gonna lie and wasn't gonna let them down." Remembering the incident years later, Shuttlesworth confessed that "my language probably wasn't as sweet as could be." But following that meeting there was no doubt who the real force behind the Birmingham campaign was. King might have been the voice of the movement, but Shuttlesworth was its bowels. A compromise was reached that allowed King to keep his promise to the merchants, while letting Shuttlesworth reserve the option of restarting the demonstrations if a satisfactory deal was not struck. "I would've died right there on that spot," Shuttlesworth said later about that pivotal moment. "If we had just called it off, without an agreement, the merchants would've said, 'We never agreed to anything.' And we would not have gotten a victory. And King's name would be mud now instead of immortal."

PROGRESS AND DENIAL

Just as the jails became stuffed beyond capacity, a deal was hammered out with the merchants that promised limited desegregation of stores and eating establishments, the release of all the demonstrators still in jail, gradual hiring of black salesclerks, and the eventual formation of an interracial alliance committed to the improvement of the city's race relations. In fact, the concessions from the white leaders fell far short of the SCLC's original goals. King's "compromise," however, would be framed for the world as a resounding victory for the civil rights movement. And that perception of victory, however hollow, would ultimately lead to several legitimate triumphs. The announcement was made on May 10.

Birmingham native Diane McWhorter's Pulitzer Prize–winning opus, *Carry Me Home*, gives a sweeping history of her hometown during the civil rights era. In a 2004 television interview she explained why King's strategy in the city was ultimately so effective. "The Chamber of Commerce made a deal with King in 1963 to end the demonstrations because it was just killing the city economically," said McWhorter. Many of Birmingham's white business owners would rely upon the Ku Klux Klan to do their dirty work, almost like a Deep South mafia. But the exposure King's movement brought to the city was creating a pattern of diminishing returns for the businesses when it came to the Klan. Said McWhorter:

> When the Chamber of Commerce stopped using the Klan, it was because [the Klan] were doing things that got bad publicity for the city. They didn't care about the publicity as long as there was a heavy manufacturing economic base. . . . But toward the end of the 1950s when the economy started changing to a consumer and service economy, they *did* have to worry about the image of Birmingham. And the image was terrible.

When the city leaders couldn't get companies to locate their offices downtown because of all the chaos, they knew it was time to cut a deal with King. "So it was economics that drove the change of heart," said McWhorter. "And that change of heart was brought about by the civil rights movement, which created this situation where [segregation policies] became economically untenable."

This being Birmingham, however, the Ku Klux Klan (likely with some prompting from Bull Connor) had to have the final word. A day after the peace agreement was announced, Martin's brother A. D. was the recipient of a bomb blast at his Birmingham home. In addition, the room where Martin was staying at the Gaston Motel was bombed. No one was hurt in either case (Martin was home in Atlanta when the explosive went off), but it was a clear signal that Birmingham's segregationist forces would not go down easily.

Sadly, things did not end as well for the four little girls who were killed by a bomb blast later that year, on September 15, as they attended Sunday school at Sixteenth Street Baptist Church. The church building was located across the street from Kelly Ingram Park, which had been ground zero for some of the spring campaign's ugliest moments. The murder of the four girls delivered a stark message that Birmingham's white-supremacist faction would not exit the stage quietly. This too would become a critical chapter in the Birmingham story.

Shuttlesworth later recalled the devastation of the church bombing. He knew it was both a sign of the movement's progress and the Klan's way of reminding them that the white man was still in charge. "They felt like we were making some headway," he said. "It was tragic, but in every war innocent people get killed." Shuttlesworth said President Kennedy had first framed it for him in terms of warfare. During a visit to the White House, Shuttlesworth told him, "Mr. Kennedy, those girls were in Sunday school, studying the Bible." He remembered the president's reply: "Reverend Shuttlesworth, as tragic as it is, in every war, some people have to die." But Shuttlesworth suspected this was also the key to their ultimate triumph in

Birmingham. "Maybe that's why we win," he said, "because Dr. King always said that unearned suffering has to be redemptive."

In later years people would compare the events that took place on the streets and sidewalks of Birmingham to other hallowed battle sites. They were just as important as Valley Forge or Gettysburg or Antietam, remarked the late David Vann, a white attorney who was a member of the city's reform movement during the 1963 protests and who would later serve as Birmingham's mayor in the 1970s. It took some time, however, before Vann could recognize Birmingham 1963 as the revolution it was. Initially, he counted himself among the gradualists who wanted to wait for the process of reform to play out under newly elected Mayor Albert Boutwell.

Like the Birmingham Eight, Vann recalled being disheartened by Martin Luther King Jr.'s unwanted intrusion into the city's affairs. "I wasn't mad at Dr. King because he made Birmingham look bad," he said. "I was upset with Dr. King because he wouldn't give us a chance to prove what we could do through the political processes." He added that both white and black leaders in the city had put themselves on the line to displace Bull Connor and get Boutwell elected. They wanted to prove that good people could use the democratic process to change things. But King and his movement were tired of waiting.

Vann eventually realized that what King did in Birmingham was much bigger than Birmingham. "I became philosophical about it later and realized that King's campaign wasn't a campaign against Birmingham," he said. "It was a campaign not even against the South. It was a campaign against America. Because what was done by law in Alabama was done de facto in New York and Chicago and Detroit and San Francisco and throughout this country."

Today Janice Kelsey is a director of ministry and community development at her brother's church. Like her brother, she had also worked as an educator in Birmingham's schools before settling at Greater Shiloh Baptist. She spent a total of three days in jail during those fateful events of 1963. When she talks about those days, you can hear the pride crackling in her voice. "I'm glad I took a stand," she says. "I had no idea how far-reaching the effects of it would be. I did not do it just for myself, but for my children and my grand-children." She takes a deep breath. "Yes, I was a part of something that made a difference—not just in Birmingham, but across the nation and around the world."

A YEAR THAT MATTERED

The Sixteenth Street church-bombing tragedy notwithstanding, the Birmingham campaign ultimately would go down as a stunning success, a game-changer that marked a new momentum in the black civil rights movement. The events in the city attracted important national media coverage and thus captured the attention of an American public that could not fully fathom the ferocity of racial segregation and hatred that existed in the American South.

The campaign was crucial for gaining national support among American citizens and the Kennedy administration, which one historian noted had "perfected the arts of delay and denial" as it attempted to curry support among Southern Democrats while taking incremental steps toward change. The Birmingham effort would also help pave the way for King's August 1963 March on Washington, with its 250,000 marchers descending on the nation's capital; his 1964 Nobel Peace Prize honor; as well as President Lyndon Johnson's signing of the 1964 Civil Rights Act. Moreover, Birmingham emboldened the movement to embark on the tumultuous Selma to Montgomery marches that would lead to the 1965 Voting Rights Act. *Time* magazine, which had earlier chastised King for poking his nose in Birmingham's business, would wind up declaring him its 1963 "Man of the

Year." None of it would have been possible without King and the SCLC's successful stand in the Magic City.

Coming during a year that would also cast a long shadow over the nation with the assassinations of NAACP leader Medgar Evers on June 12 and President Kennedy on November 22, the Birmingham campaign stands out as one of the key turning points in an era filled with momentous trials, tribulations and triumphs. Twenty-six years earlier in her 1937 novel, *Their Eyes Were Watching God*, Zora Neale Hurston observed wistfully, "There are years that ask questions and years that answer." Birmingham 1963 was a year that did plenty of both.

Dreams and Nightmares

On January 15, 2006, which would have been Martin Luther King Jr.'s seventy-seventh birthday, the Cartoon Network aired an episode of *The Boondocks* animated series that, depending on your point of view, could make you laugh until you cry or cry *because* you're laughing. Titled "Return of the King," the episode confronts viewers with the question, *What would Martin Luther King Jr. say about the state of black America if he were alive today?* The answer, for *Boondocks* creator Aaron McGruder at least, is not a cheery one.

When it debuted as a newspaper comic strip in 1999, *The Boondocks* quickly earned a reputation as one of the most trenchant sources of social commentary on race in America. Never short on controversial topics, Aaron McGruder's iconoclastic satire about the misadventures of two African American brothers transplanted from the inner city to the suburbs to live with their grandfather stirred some to nod their heads in recognition and others to shake their heads in irritation. Readers always felt something. When the comic strip came to television in 2005, many believed McGruder's creation lost a step in the translation. But however one may judge the show's overall value, the "Return of the King" episode should be required viewing for anyone concerned about Dr. King's legacy or about the future of black America.

In the story, the show's precocious narrator, ten-year-old Huey Freeman, dreams that King was not killed but critically wounded in 1968. After falling into a coma for more than three decades, King awakes to a world filled with one disturbing sight after another. Now bald and visibly aged, King walks along a city street that happens to bear his name. When gunshots ring out, causing the gathered crowd to flee, King learns one of his first hard lessons about the twenty-first century: "streets named after him weren't the very safest." The climactic moment occurs during what was supposed to be a movement rally at a church that ends up becoming the site of a riotous party filled with every sort of modern-day black stereotype—young men fighting and drinking, young women in skin-tight clothes bumping and grinding, no one apparently aware of how shiftless and lost they are.

King approaches the pulpit and attempts to wrest control of the proceedings, but the crowd is too consumed in its reveling to hear him. As Huey's voiceover puts it, "King looked over his people and saw they were in great need." Finally, having reached his breaking point, the weary civil rights leader drops all formalities and speaks to the people in a language he believes they will understand: "Will you ignorant niggas please shut the hell up?" he shouts in his familiar preacherly cadence. The partying comes to a screeching halt. "Is this it?" King continues. "*This* is what I got all those ass whoopings for?" He then launches into an extended rant, lecturing and rebuking the crowd for its pathological behavior and its failure to live up to the ideals he had dreamed about forty years earlier. By the end, it's clear that King sees no hope for this generation. He concludes, "I've seen what's around the corner, I've seen what's over the horizon, and I promise you, you niggas have nothing to celebrate! And no, I won't get there with you. I'm going to Canada."

The crowd stands in stunned silence as the iconic preacher exits the church.

It's difficult to watch "Return of the King" without comparing the young people portrayed there (albeit in animated drawings) with the teens and young adults who, for the sake of freedom, exposed themselves to physical harm and possible arrest at lunch counters, bus stations and in the streets of Birmingham. Today many young people are fighting and going to jail for entirely different reasons. The irony hurts.

Reactions to the *Boondocks* episode were decidedly mixed. Some latter-day civil rights activists came down hard on the Cartoon Network and McGruder for portraying King as an N-word-spouting critic of the black community's foibles. They demanded an apology. On the other hand, the episode won the prestigious Peabody Award for "distinguished achievement and meritorious public service" by a television program. The controversy is emblematic of many of the challenges facing the black community today, including the inability by some to engage in honest self-critique with an eye toward improvement and correction. But wrapped within that larger concern is the equally troubling matter of what to make of King's legacy today.

THE FORGOTTEN KING

During my preparation for this book, I asked several friends to share with me their thoughts about King's legacy and ways that it has affected them. Jennifer Parker, an African American writer and educator from Jackson, Mississippi, volunteered a story about an experience with students from her eighth-grade language arts class. "I was a new teacher, working in an 'at risk' school where the enrollment was ninety-eight percent African American and predominantly poor," Jennifer told me. One year, as the MLK holiday approached, the school's principal spoke over the intercom, describing her idea for a schoolwide essay contest in honor of the occasion. She insisted that every student take part and promised to award and put on display the best essays responding to the theme "What Martin Luther King Jr.'s Dream Means to Me." Jennifer recalled that most of her students didn't pay attention, so she had to go over the assignment a second time. "I managed to get about thirty-percent participation by prodding them with bribe of extra credit." She hadn't expected literary gems, but Jennifer figured an inspirational figure such as Dr. King might strike a chord with her students. The resulting essays were disappointing. "Even the better efforts were full of clichés, superficial repetition, and scant or altogether faulty historical information," she said. "The most profound statement I encountered in reading their papers was, 'Martin Luther King was a great man who dreamed for people to get freedom and have civil rights, so he made a lot of speeches and marched until he got shot.'" Jennifer was saddened that, even after several years of Black History Month assignments and book reports on MLK biographies, her students knew only the most oft-repeated generalities about King's life.

I should add that Jennifer also shared more uplifting memories of growing up in the 1970s and 1980s with a portrait of King on the living room wall and being in awe of the stories about the civil rights movement that her parents and grandparents would tell her. Perhaps this is why she was so distraught about a younger generation's fast-fading awareness of who King was. "If I sound disillusioned, please chalk it up to a green educator's hurt pride," she said. "I am still embarrassed about having failed to inspire those students more with a love of learning and a sense of the privilege they enjoy today because of earlier generations." She no longer takes for granted that young African Americans are coming to her with a readymade understanding of Martin Luther King Jr.'s significance. Instead, she has accepted the important responsibility of retelling the stories—just as her relatives did for her—to make sure they know.

In various ways, King has been sanitized, domesticated or simply forgotten. The real Baptist churchman and fighter for social justice has been reduced to the fatherly saint who "had a dream." Conservatives who once reviled him now claim him as one of their own (at least when it comes to select issues). Liberals who once failed to fully grasp his significance now treat him as their modern standard-bearer while ignoring his roots in the church. But all these versions of King pale in comparison to the radical visionary who composed "Letter from Birmingham Jail." Revisionist history abounds, but somehow the real man has been misplaced.

"It's easy to forget how despised King was in his own time by many on the right and the left, by many within the church and outside it," says West Virginia Wesleyan College religion professor Debra Dean Murphy. "As the frequency of his public speeches increased toward the end of his life so did his visible, palpable rage." Indeed, a common mistake in reviewing historical figures is to freeze them in one era or event of their lives and treat it as the entirety of their existence. For our memories of King, homing in on the friendlier parts of "I Have a Dream" is how most choose to remember him. But what about the King who lived and marched in Chicago, drawing vicious mobs of white protesters? What about the King who, after a lengthy silence, felt compelled to speak out on the tragedy of the Vietnam War and the disproportionate toll it took on minorities and the poor? What about the King who frequently doubted white America's willingness to leave behind its systemic uses of racism and oppression of the poor?

Malcolm X was often portrayed as King's militant rival, but many historians now argue that the actual distance between the two men became less pronounced as Malcolm grew more disillusioned with the Nation of Islam's black militancy and Martin became more despondent over America's unwillingness to move toward the beloved community.

Murphy believes our "I Have a Dream" inertia deprives us of encountering the more radical, full-color King from his later years. She adds, "As his preaching evolved in his last years, he moved from what one observer called a 'homiletics of identification' to a 'homiletics of confrontation.' The radical politics that King envisioned—for the church and the nation—did not endear him to either; it got him killed."

MARCH TO MEMPHIS

Despite ongoing struggles with depression and insomnia, King continued to keep a packed schedule, accepting most invitations that came his way. This only exacerbated the heavy stress he was enduring. In early 1968 King was working to organize a massive Poor People's Campaign in Washington for both Negroes and whites. But in late March he interrupted planning for the campaign to respond to a crisis in Memphis, Tennessee, where Negro sanitation workers were striking for equal pay and better working conditions.

The anger and hostility he had been encountering at different protest events, particularly in the large cities, began to visibly erode King's spirit. Though he didn't fear death—in fact, he routinely predicted he would die young—it was impossible for him, a mortal man, not to be anxious. As he participated in each march through usually hostile environments, he probably flashed back to the bombings of his home in Montgomery, or the 1958 incident in Harlem during a book signing where a mentally disturbed black woman plunged a letter opener into his chest, nearly puncturing his aorta. How could he not be anxious? How could he not, on some level, figure that eventually his time would come? "This is a sick society," he had told Coretta following the announcement of President Kennedy's assassination. "This is what is going to happen to me."

In the late 1990s I had the chance to conduct a brief interview with King's trusted SCLC lieutenant Andrew Young, who would go on to serve as mayor of Atlanta, a U.S. Congressman, and a UN ambassador. Young was visiting the University of Chicago during a tour to promote his spiritual memoir, *A Way Out of No Way*. According to Young, one way that King dealt with the overwhelming pressures on him was through laughter. He explained how King would joke with his inner circle of preacher friends in the SCLC about what he would say at their funerals if they should happened to be killed during the next campaign.

"He did not take himself seriously at all," said Young.

> And he wouldn't let you take yourself seriously. The way he made us deal with our fears was he'd say, "Somebody's going to get killed in Birmingham. And if it's you, Abernathy, I will preach the best eulogy ever preached over a brother." And then he'd start preaching the eulogy about you. Saying all the embarrassing things you wouldn't want said.

Young explained King would have them laughing so hard they wouldn't have time to be afraid.

But that laughing King is not the one we see in the public images from Memphis. As Anderson School of Theology scholar and King friend James Earl Massey observes, "In the pictures of him marching, you can see the grimmest look on his face. He was very tense. And the speech he gave the night before his death reveals how much he was expecting hostility to rise against him."

On that night, April 3, 1968, a violent thunderstorm drenched Memphis as a somber-looking Martin Luther King Jr. took the stage at the Mason Temple, denominational headquarters of the Church of God in Christ. Despite the furious rain, an enthusiastic crowd of two thousand people had gathered to hear King. After an impassioned appeal to the audience to continue the work the movement had begun, King's address concluded on an eerie note. He spoke of the hard road ahead, his wish to live a long life, but his understanding that he wouldn't. He had "been to the mountaintop," however, and he knew the black community would someday reach "the Promised Land" with or without him. He just wanted to do God's will. King, in effect, had preached his own funeral—one day before his death.

The next evening the thirty-nine-year-old Baptist preacher was shot down as he stood on the second-floor balcony of Memphis's Lorraine Motel.

REBOOTING KING'S LEGACY

In Martin Luther King Jr.'s 1967 book *Where Do We Go from Here: Chaos or Community?* which would be his last, he wrote: "Whites, it must frankly be said, are not putting in a mass effort to re-educate themselves out of their racial ignorance. . . . It is an aspect of their sense of superiority that the white people of America believe they have so little to learn." King's tone represented a more radical, certainly more despondent version of the critique of America he had offered four years earlier in "Letter from Birmingham Jail."

In a vicious political climate that would seize upon an ancient, out-of-context sound bite from President Obama's former pastor, Jeremiah Wright, to both destroy Wright and bring down Obama by association, hearing King say something like that is stunning. After all, in their social-media criticisms of Wright, many whites wondered why he couldn't be more like Dr. King, "a real Christian." Never mind that when King was alive, and for years after his death, many would not acknowledge him as a *real* Christian; if King were to say something similar today, he'd be called a racist and drummed out of town. It's a sign of how potent the amnesiac powers of time are that we don't remember how ticked off King was at the intransigence of the white community during the last years of his life.

Debra Dean Murphy, who is white, points out that as far back as 1957 King was saying things such as "we can't solve our problems now until there is a radical redistribution of economic and political power." She also notes that a sermon King had planned to preach the week that he was killed was titled "Why America May Go to Hell."

Says Murphy:

> We still can't absorb his real words. We prefer the "other" MLK—the one who affirms our own pious outrage at racial inequality. But when King insists that such inequality is inextricably linked to an economic system that makes our comfortable lives possible, even as it debases and erases the marginalized and dispossessed, we get nervous. We don't want the justice that King dreamed of to cost us anything.

So, instead of abandoning our unjust systems, we dilute and defuse the words of the prophet. And over time, we turn him into a fiction.

My friend Jerald January shared a story with me that reveals the perils of reducing King to a harmless dreamer. In the mid-1980s, as an urban youth minister, Jerald and a partner led a weekly life-skills workshop for the male students at a Denver high school. The school was 60 percent black and mostly poor. "Their grades were horrible, and many of them didn't have fathers in their lives," recalls Jerald. "So we wanted to provide a place for them to ask questions and learn how to be men." When they started the program, Jerald and his partner were hoping to attract twelve students each week; they got eighty-three.

During one session, Jerald realized the value of the workshop after asking the students where they would go if they could take a trip anywhere in the world. When one of the students said, "Colorado Springs," which was just seventy miles away, Jerald discovered that at sixteen and seventeen years old many of the students had never left their Denver zip code. "Without thinking, I volunteered to take anyone who earned a 2.5 GPA on their report card on a trip around the country for eight days to visit colleges and experience culture." It was one of those moments, says Jerald, where his mouth ran faster than his brain. But after a series of providential circumstances allowed them to raise the funds needed for travel, food and lodging, he knew God had inspired him to make the impulsive offer.

Fifty of the students were able to make the trip, and the group's travels went smoothly. They explored colleges and touristy sites in Oklahoma, Alabama, and Georgia. In Atlanta, the group visited the Morehouse campus, the underground mall, and ate plenty of chicken and grits. Their final stop before heading back to Colorado was the King Center. "But there was one kid who should have never gotten on the bus," Jerald recalls pensively. "I'll call him 'Stephen.'" He was seventeen years old, six-feet-four and very handsome, but he was a troubled young man. Originally from Harlem, his family had moved to Denver to get him away from the gangbanger life that he had fallen into on the East Coast. "The truth is, his GPA was only 2.1, so he shouldn't have gone with us," says Jerald. "But there was just something in him that led us to make an exception." Exhausted from the long week of travel, Jerald was looking forward to returning home. But he also was excited about giving his students a chance to explore important American history at the King Center. "We got off the bus to do the tour, but first the kids wanted to see Dr. King's tomb." The stone sepulcher, which sits in the middle of a large reflecting pool, is inscribed with Dr. King's legendary words "Free at last, Free at last." Jerald hung back at a distance as the kids ran to take pictures, but after a few minutes he saw some sort of commotion taking place near the tomb area. "My first thought was that Stephen had finally snapped and gotten into a fight with someone. I said to myself, *Lord, this Negro has jumped on somebody right in front of Dr. King's grave.*" Jerald jostled his way through the crowd as quickly as he could. All the while he heard a loud wailing, as if someone was in great pain. Finally, arriving at the tomb, he saw Stephen—but he wasn't fighting.

He was sitting hunched over at the edge of the pool, trembling and crying uncontrollably. Several of the other boys stood around him, nervously patting him on the head or touching his shoulders to calm him down.

"Hey, man, what's wrong with you?" Jerald asked, stooping beside him.

Stephen looked up and tried to catch his breath to speak. "I didn't believe it, Mr. January," he said between sobs. "I didn't believe it."

"You didn't believe what?"

Stephen pointed to King's tomb behind him. "I didn't believe there was a real Martin Luther King. I thought they made him up. Mr. January, he was *real*."

It still moves Jerald to tears of his own to think about it today. This young man's existence had been so isolated and cut off from a sense of optimism and hope that he couldn't wrap his mind around the notion that someone like Martin Luther King Jr. actually existed in the real world. Jerald says the experience changed Stephen forever. The following school year, he wore a shirt and tie every day. He raised his GPA to a 3.0, earned a scholarship to a Texas university and went on to major in business. "He suddenly realized that he was *somebody*," says Jerald. "That he was a real person, too—just like Dr. King."

A closer study of Dr. King's life, beyond the obligatory "I Have a Dream" sound bites, might go a long way toward helping us reclaim that *real* person—the man who met Jesus in his kitchen in Montgomery, failed miserably in Albany, but penetrated the soul of America in Birmingham.

After the Revolution

Martin Luther King Jr.

In the fall of 1963, on a jetliner zooming from Atlanta to Los Angeles, Martin Luther King Jr. sat quietly, peering outside from his window seat. He was drinking in the view of the Appalachian Mountains below when the plane suddenly bounced and jerked in a fit of turbulence. King looked up from his pillow, flashed a playful smile at the *Time* magazine reporter seated beside him and said, "I guess that's Birmingham down below."

Today if King were to fly over Birmingham, he would find friendlier skies. But I still would advise him to keep his seatbelt fastened.

In a city once governed by white supremacists, there has now been a thirty-year custom of electing African American mayors. The city's airport is named after the Rev. Fred Shuttlesworth. In the downtown district, not far from where attack dogs and fire hoses once assailed nonviolent protesters, stands the Birmingham Civil Rights Institute. Inside this sobering museum of a not-so-distant America, visitors can review the artifacts of the Birmingham revolution and actually touch the bars of the jail cell that housed King during his famous imprisonment. To the Institute's west stands the remains of the Gaston Motel, where King and the SCLC established their base of operations during the 1963 campaign. To the west stands Sixteenth Street Baptist Church, where the four little girls became victims of white supremacist terrorism on a September Sunday morning. To the north sits Kelly Ingram Park, which is now filled with statues and sculptures capturing moments from the dramatic 1963 showdown between Bull Connor's cops and firemen and King's nonviolent throng of protesters. Throughout the downtown streets are official signs marking various milestones from the movement. One leaves the city feeling that it is all remarkably well done, until you step back and realize: the entire downtown is actually a memorial to 1963. To walk the streets of Birmingham is to experience a city that, instead of denying it or playing it down, embraces its painful history. The result is, frankly, quite morbid. There's nothing light about a tour of downtown Birmingham. When I explored those streets in April 2012, they were eerily vacant. Walking where protesters marched is surreal. But the uneasiness you feel is important. It's necessary. One senses that the city is working out the tragedy of its past in real time.

A MOUNTAIN RUNS THROUGH IT

"Things are better here today racially, but it's by no means settled," says Tracy Hipps, executive director of the Christian Service Mission, a faith-based community development organization in Birmingham. Fifty years after the 1963 campaign, he believes the current mayor, William Bell, and other city leaders are doing a good job of honoring the city's history while trying to move forward. "There is certainly improvement," he says. "But it's challenging. There's a culture here that's hard to crack."

For Hipps, the best way to explain the immensity of the challenge facing Birmingham is to point to Red Mountain, a vast and scenic ridge that runs diagonally, southwest to northeast, through the metropolitan area. A spillover of the rugged terrain that forms the Appalachian Mountains, Birmingham's Red Mountain represents a natural boundary between the area's urban and suburban residents—which means it's not only an emblem of geography and nature but also of race and class, with most of the predominantly white middle-class population living over the hills in affluent communities while most African Americans scramble for progress in the struggling inner city below. Just the idea of it flabbergasts Tracy Hipps. "That mountain is a *real* barrier," he says, suggesting that it's both a physical and cultural obstacle to unity in Birmingham. "We have one of the greatest places for learning about the civil rights movement with the Civil Rights Institute, and I would say that out of 1.3 million people in the area, most African Americans have gone to it—not to mention visitors from all over the United States. But I would daresay that 95 percent of Birmingham's white suburban community has never been there and frankly don't see the need for it. For me, that's a reflection of where we're at." People always want to say it's getting better, Hipps balks, "but they're not willing to do some actions that actually move us forward and bring learning and 'break down the walls that divide us,' as the Scriptures say."

A South Carolina native, Hipps moved to Birmingham in 1980 to attend Southeastern Bible College. He worked as an inner-city missionary in Chicago for six years before returning to Birmingham in 1990 to work at an all-black church. The soul of the Magic City had gotten in his blood, he discovered. In many ways, it was a continuation of his childhood experience. "When I was in junior high in South Carolina, integration was put in place and I was bused to an all-black middle school where I was beat up, discriminated against and put in a bad situation." His negative encounters with African Americans did nothing to reverse the ugly stereotypes that he had been conditioned to believe. "My dad taught me that every black person is bad. . . . I literally was taught to be a racist." His voice, soaked in a no-nonsense southern drawl, begins to crack. "I'm a recovering racist," he says. "That means I was made to move past it, but I'm struggling still."

Hipps's rehab from racism was not simple, but he believes it became inevitable when he seriously committed his life to God. "From your family you're taught how to act toward people, but the Word of God breaks through even that. If you honestly try to live out the Word—Jew, Greek, it doesn't matter who you are—the Word of God will transform you." As a teen, he began to develop relationships with "the people I was supposed to hate," and things progressed from there. He moved to Birmingham and worked in juvenile detention centers. He worked with Latino and African American students in Chicago. He now leads a multiracial organization that works to break down walls and create partnerships between churches and individuals in the Birmingham community. "With Christian Service Mission (CSM), we want to bring together groups that ordinarily wouldn't work with each other—black, white, Hispanic, rich, poor." And despite major dividing points, Hipps has found success in bridging the urban-suburban separation by offering "work projects and compassion outreach" opportunities that allow different groups to serve together.

One of CSM's success stories is the relationship that was forged between Greater Shiloh Baptist in the city and Shades Mountain Baptist, one of the largest churches in the suburbs. The congregations have exchanged choirs, partnered on work projects and are planning a joint mission trip to India. "Shades Mountain's pastor Danny Wood and I have developed a valuable camaraderie that I think is mutual and genuine," says Greater Shiloh Baptist's Michael Wesley. "The learning curve on both sides has been elevated, we're learning from each other."

Hipps relishes bringing pastors and churches together, but he also knows that his focus on racial reconciliation cannot end on the job; it must play out in his personal life as well. "I have college-age kids," he says, "and I'm trying to raise them without the prejudice that I inherited. That's the legacy of change that I want to pass on to the next generation."

Tracy Hipps's brazen but sincere personality brings to mind the spirit of a Fred Shuttlesworth, who in his day was unafraid to tell it like it is. Hipps, for example, pushes back against the popular notion among white Christians that we should bypass racial issues by being "colorblind," which he believes can become an excuse for ignoring the elephant in the room—or in Birmingham's case, the mountain. "I *do* see color," he says. "I see every color, and God sees color because he *made* color. But the difference don't make a difference." He adds softly, "Dr. King started a movement here fifty years ago, and I'm here to help continue it."

WHOLE CHURCH, WHOLE CITY

Today, the erstwhile "Pittsburgh of the South" is still Alabama's largest city, but it no longer specializes in steel and manufacturing. Instead, service industries and medical research groups now dominate the economy. If one believes the P.R. from the city's official website, Birmingham is "one of the nation's most livable cities with a vibrant downtown, a burgeoning loft community, a world-class culinary scene and more green space per capita than any other city in the nation!" It is hard to dismiss the natural beauty of the area—the sweeping Appalachian foothills and lush vistas. But then there's the matter of that pesky racial history. It looms as wide as Red Mountain.

Birmingham suffers from profound racial fissures like any other American city, says Kevin Moore, the executive director of Mission Birmingham, "but our history makes it stand out even more." Like Tracy Hipps, Moore runs a faith-based nonprofit that's working to unite the city's faith community across racial and cultural lines.

"According to some statistics, Birmingham is one of the most evangelized cities in the U.S.," he says. "You're apt to hear someone share the gospel with you at any moment." Yet, he says, the city's deep religious roots belie its racial partitions.

Listening to Hipps and Moore, two white Christian leaders striving to bring change in a city fraught with racial baggage, one is confronted with the realization that much of the Birmingham story is inaccurate—at least the one we get on the outside. From a distance, one of the positive narratives we hear is of the city's evolution from segregationist stronghold to civil rights beacon. There's work to be done, we're told, but overall it's a story of hope and forward movement. But the problem with that storyline is that it doesn't begin to convey the grim implications of that darn mountain. And, sadly, depending on which side of the mountain you're on, you may not even care.

A major complication facing those trying to bring unity to Birmingham is the city's intractable political structure, says Moore. "We live in a seven-county metropolitan statistical area, with about ninety-eight different municipalities in it, and none of them are in unity with each other. There's a complete disconnect." For Moore, this urban-suburban fragmentation is a reflection of the region's lingering racial divisions.

Michael Wesley agrees. "The challenge is with the municipal governments," he says. "The city of Birmingham is one municipality, but there are numerous other municipalities all around it—but they're separated from the city." From his perspective the southern cities that have made the most progress over the last fifty years—Atlanta, Nashville, Charlotte, Jacksonville—have found ways to bring a measure of unity to their metro areas. "All of those cities were on par with Birmingham in terms of size and municipalities at one time," he explains, "but they were able to dissolve the individual municipalities to create a metroplex and have a central form of government that impacts the outlying areas, and as a result they've been able to move forward." Pastor Wesley believes "there's going to be a great, great deal of challenge" before that kind of consolidation happens in the Birmingham area, if it ever does. The greatest impediment, he says, is economic. "I don't envision suburban Vestavia Hills or Mount Brook—which at one point was listed among the top ten wealthiest communities in America— giving up their strongholds. They have separate school districts that they're proud of and good city services. I don't imagine them giving that up to become more unified with Birmingham proper." And that, he adds, "is where the racial challenge is going to remain for Birmingham."

Moore sees the problem aggravated by the white population's cynical view of Birmingham's predominantly African American leadership. "I think there's a feeling from the white majority culture in the suburbs that Birmingham's black city leaders don't know what they're doing," he confesses. "They'll point out that we're the seventh most dangerous city in the United States according to FBI stats. They'll point to the fact that the public schools have been taken over by the state of Alabama because the local school board was so extremely dysfunctional." From the white perspective, he says, there's a feeling the city will never get its act together. "So they adopt a 'hands off' attitude about it of 'let the city do what it does.' But the problem with that is that we're a metro area; we're connected to each other."

On the other hand, Moore suspects that a few African American city leaders sometimes try to exploit Birmingham's race issue "as a means for gain—either as an advantage politically, financially, or in terms of power." And that just exacerbates the problem, he says. "Fortunately, Mayor Bell is committed to the issue of unity and has done a good job of trying to stay connected to the leadership across the metro area," Moore adds, positively.

Kevin Moore grew up near Detroit, went to college in Chattanooga and came to Birmingham in 1983 for his first job out of college. He's been there ever since. In addition to leading Mission Birmingham's efforts in the inner city, he's also the worship pastor at Shades Mountain Independent Church in the suburbs. As a Christian trying to build bridges between communities, he has been permitted an intimate view of both sides of the mountain. And he reserves hope that the two sides can come together. One of the ways he has seen it happen is through the annual Pastors' Prayer Summit sponsored by Mission Birmingham that has brought together dozens of local church leaders since 1998. The racially and denominationally mixed fellowship also has led to numerous friendships across the Red Mountain divide. Says Moore, "A passion of the group is worship-based prayer, where you're speaking the words of Scripture and praying back to God what he's communicating to us." In November 2012 the group decided to "pray through" King's "Letter from Birmingham Jail." "It was a powerful exercise in hearing God through the voice of Martin Luther King," Moore says. "The letter is itself is an amazing document, but the power of joining with a diverse group of leaders to pray in agreement with it, utilizing its language and vision. . . . It was a remarkable experience."

Moore still thinks Birmingham's divisions are formidable—not only racially and economically, but generationally: he observes that the intra-racial philosophical clashes between the city's older and younger African American ministers are sometimes just as huge as the black-white divide. But he's prepared to keep pushing. "Our vision is to see Birmingham transformed," he says. "The whole church taking the whole gospel to the whole city." As Fred Shuttlesworth suggested five decades earlier, if they can pull it off here, the other places will be easy.

THE WAY TO RECONCILIATION

The stone gateway at the southwest corner of Kelly Ingram Park is inscribed with the words: "Place of Revolution and Reconciliation." The revolution is a historical truth, and there are many emblems of its factualness spread throughout the city. But *reconciliation*?

What historian Warren Goldstein likes about the epigram at Kelly Ingram Park is that it doesn't stop at "revolution." A successful movement must have reconciliation as well. And this is what set Dr. King's approach apart from others, he says. "It's not enough just to be a place of revolution. There have been plenty of revolutions in the world, but when the victors end up chopping the heads off the losers, that's all people remember. But the beauty of nonviolent direct action is that it was the only tactic that had the chance of converting the people on the other side."

Conversions can be long and drawn-out affairs, however. And sometimes you have no assurance that they'll ever come. Like most places in the United States when it comes to racial unity and social justice, one suspects "reconciliation" is still a work in progress in Birmingham. But the city is at least transparent about it. It has to be. Its history is too infamous to hide.

Another unusual homage to the city's legacy was conceived in 1997 by James Rotch, a white Birmingham attorney. While traveling on a business trip, Rotch jotted down his personal commitment "to recognize the importance of every individual, regardless of race or color." His six-point creed, aimed at "eliminating racism in the world one person at a time," became the rallying cry of a grassroots movement. "The Birmingham Pledge" was formally introduced to the public in 1998, and since then has been used in classrooms and educational programs around the globe. The movement's most conspicuous manifestation is a fifty-foot mural displaying text from the pledge on an exterior wall of the Birmingham police headquarters. The colorful image, designed by a local high school student, features four youths of different ethnicities expressing their friendship. The full-circle irony of a public facility that once jailed Negro children en masse now promoting a message of racial inclusivity is unavoidable. The "Birmingham Pledge" reportedly has been signed—on paper and online—by more than 120,000 people from around the world. It even has its own nonprofit foundation. With words echoing the lofty principles espoused by Dr. King, the pledge phenomenon also calls to mind King's media savvy. Indeed, one wonders if Bull Connor's reign would have been shorter had the Internet been around in the 1960s.

Still, despite the visible evolution of the city from a Jim Crow stronghold to a community trying hard to redeem its past, Diane McWhorter believes Birmingham's white residents are still too defensive about the topic of race relations in their city. "There's a rush to closure, but no one wants to go through atonement or revelation to get there," said McWhorter in 2011. "So what [white] Birmingham has tried to do is go from amnesia about all of it to closure, and you can't do that. You can't go around it; you must go through it."

King Among
the Evangelicals

WILLIAM PANNELL CANNOT RECALL whether there were six or eight African Americans on the flight, but he knew they were badly outnumbered. His group, comprised of black evangelical leaders from around the nation, had gathered in Chicago en route to Berlin. It was 1966 and they were traveling to Germany for the World Congress on Evangelism, sponsored by the Billy Graham Evangelistic Association (BGEA) in cooperation with other evangelical groups worldwide. Pannell, who at the time was a staff evangelist for Youth for Christ, was accustomed to being one of just a handful of blacks in the largely white evangelical world of the 1960s. But this event would be different.

The World Congress on Evangelism was billed as "the largest ecumenical and evangelical gathering of the Church since Pentecost." Christian leaders from almost every nation of the world were expected. As theologian James Earl Massey described it, "Learned bishops sat with outstanding lay evangelists. World-famed theologians shared insights and convictions with parish ministers. Skilled evangelists to the masses sat to listen and learn."

Pannell, along with Massey, BGEA associates Howard O. Jones

and Ralph Bell, and others represented just a few of evangelicalism's leading black voices at the time. Still, the presence of their delegation would ensure at least a bit of color from the United States.

"I deplaned at the Tegel Airport alongside Massey and Jones and one other person," recalls Pannell. "Before we could get far, we were met by a German woman who, in her shaky English, asked, 'Is Dr. King with you?' Someone out of our small group replied, 'No, he is not on board.' To which she replied, 'But he will surely be here won't he?' Not wanting to go into all sorts of history, we simply suggested that he probably would not be coming. She was clearly disappointed." Two years earlier, King had visited East and West Germany, where he spoke to small groups and enthusiastic crowds in the thousands. The woman no doubt remembered his historic visit and the inspiring messages he shared about peace, freedom and the dignity of all humanity. What she didn't understand, suspects Pannell, was the unspoken code at the time that forbade Christians of King's ilk from participating in a evangelical function such as the World Congress on Evangelism. Though there were probably many in attendance who would have welcomed his presence, many others likely would have objected.

Today, in his eighties, William Pannell flits between being retired and serving as a distinguished professor of preaching at Fuller Theological Seminary in Pasadena. The author of *My Friend, the Enemy*, a famous 1968 book about the complicated relationship between black and white evangelicals, he continues to provide not-always-welcomed critiques of the foibles of white evangelicalism. "I for one have felt that someone should give that German woman a better answer than the one we gave her that day," says Pannell. "Someone should attempt to explain to her why Dr. King is still not *on board* in any official gathering of the evangelical clan today."

Almost fifty years later, evangelicals continue to have a strained relationship with Martin Luther King Jr.

SHIELDED FROM KING

When Dr. King wrote his passionate epistle to the eight "moderate" clergymen of Birmingham, it was obvious that he was banking on some eavesdropping happening from other Christians as well. What we were supposed to hear are the reasons why justice delayed is justice denied; why an unjust law is arguably not a law at all; why King believed the church is Christ's body, but a body weakened by social neglect and bad theology. But most of all, King wanted Christians to understand that the gospel of Jesus Christ demands holistic engagement with the real world in front of them today.

In my now two-decade journey as a Christian journalist, I've spoken to people from all points on the theological spectrum and watched the opinions about King fluctuate over the years, particularly among white evangelicals. Back in the early 1990s, one had to be ever so careful about expressing any fondness for King and his ideas. And, if one did, he or she had to make it clear that it was King's inspirational platitudes about racial harmony that he liked and not King's theology or politics. Go back a bit further and you find experiences such as that of author Philip Yancey, who grew up in Atlanta in the 1950s and 1960s, and was taught to hate black people. "Folks in my church had their own name for [King]," he writes in his book *Soul Survivor*, "Martin Lucifer Coon." Yancey said it took years "for God to break the stranglehold of blatant racism in me." And he's certainly not alone. Just recently at my church I was sharing with a white thirty-something wife and mother about my latest book project on Martin Luther King Jr., and she confessed to me that she remembered the times, when she was a child, that her dad would speak of King in now embarrassingly racist terms. "At some point he changed," she told me. "Now he's able to respect Dr. King and what he stood for, but God had to work on his heart." In some ways, evangelical perceptions of King over the years can serve as a sort of measuring stick for how far we've come as a movement—and as individuals.

"It was not until graduate school studying U.S. religious history that I first read Martin Luther King Jr.'s 'Letter from Birmingham Jail' in its entirety," says Edward Blum, a professor of race and religion at San Diego State University. "Although raised in an affluent town in the northeast and an active participant in my Presbyterian church, this sacred letter was never mentioned, read, or presented to us." Blum, now in his mid-thirties, says he knew of King, and he knew of the "Dream" speech, and he even had heard about King's extramarital affairs. But the Birmingham letter had eluded him, something he now regards as tragic.

"Why was his letter kept from me? Why did we never encounter it from youth pastors who took us to Jackson, Mississippi, on mission trips or from high school history teachers who were obsessed with the injustice of the Holocaust but not Jim Crow? Why did I have to wait to be in a 'secular' space at a state university to finally read a spiritual document addressed to people white, male, and religious like me?"

Today, reflecting back, Blum interprets his isolation from that radical version of King as a kind of conspiracy. "I can only conclude that the religious and cultural structures of the evangelicalism I was a part of, and the type of schooling we received, were built—accidentally perhaps—to shield me from knowing the depths of my nation's sins." At the same time, Blum says he was "separated from the type of spiritual resources that would've offered me ways to join God and God's people against injustices like segregation, racism, and sexism."

NOT ON THE SAME PAGE

In 1998 the late Glen Kehrein shared with me a story that, for him, symbolized the problem with evangelicals when it comes to their relationship with Martin Luther King Jr. and civil rights. Kehrein, the founder and executive director of Circle Urban Ministries in Chicago for more than thirty years before his death in 2011, spoke about his experience as a white evangelical who was denied the cultural freedom to encounter King in his fullness.

As a student at Chicago's Moody Bible Institute in September 1968, he recalled attending a campus retreat at a Baptist camping and conference center three hours north of the Windy City in Wisconsin. Sharing the huge camp grounds with Moody that year were Ralph Abernathy, Jesse Jackson and other leaders from the Southern Christian Leadership Conference. It was just five months after the murder of their leader, Dr. King, and the SCLC associates were at the center to recover and regroup for the future. Kehrein was familiar with a few of the SCLC's surviving leaders, but King had intrigued him the most. He had heard about King's reputation as a "communist" and troublemaker, and evangelical leaders had warned him about the dangerous theology contained in King's "social gospel." Kehrein didn't know what to believe. After King's murder, the streets of Chicago had turned into a war zone. The sounds and sights of gunfire and buildings engulfed in flames were fresh in his head. Even the relationships between black and white students at Moody seemed to carry an added strain. "I saw the racial divide vividly in the dorm when King's shooting was announced," Kehrein remembered. "There was a completely different reaction between the blacks and whites. We were not on the same page."

In Wisconsin, Kehrein wanted to put those disturbing matters out of his head. But he somehow knew they were matters he needed to confront. So, he was hopeful when his professor announced that Ralph Abernathy had agreed to share a few words with the Moody students. He felt that King's closest colleague might be able to give some context to his confusion about race in America. He soon discovered just how deep the confusion went.

"Dr. Abernathy completed his talk and entertained questions from my class," said Kehrein. "But with all that history in the room, and all that had transpired in the civil rights movement over the last ten years, the majority of questions we ended up asking him were about his 'personal salvation' and his understanding of the conservative tenets of evangelical doctrine." Looking back at that day, Kehrein was ashamed. "Dr. Abernathy was gracious and attempted to accommodate all our questions, but we were clueless. I think our narrow focus said a lot about the evangelical mindset during that era."

MAKING PEACE WITH KING

For years after King's death, many white Christians continued to eye him with suspicion, even as families like mine proudly displayed his portrait on our walls. Today, in an era when all fifty U.S. states now observe the King holiday and a resplendent monument to the man stands in our nation's capital, it's difficult to conceive of a time when King wasn't acceptable. But once upon a time, we couldn't hear King's prophetic voice due to all the distortion drowning it out—some of it manufactured out of racism and ignorance, some of it real: *"He was not a true Christian." "He was a communist." "He was a plagiarist." "He was an adulterer."*

Now, to their credit, many of today's evangelical leaders have learned how to view King's failures and successes in the context of his humanity. He wrestled with feelings of guilt over having too many material possessions (occasionally to the chagrin of Coretta), and his infidelity no doubt contributed to his ongoing struggles with despondency and his self-described "troubled soul." And as he neared his early death, which he seemed to know was inevitable, his tortured soul became even more evident. Yet this too forced King to be even more dependent on prayer and empowerment by God.

"It was precisely in King's humanness, his own moral frailty that his prophetic witness derived much of its moral force," contends Debra Dean Murphy. "His personal failings—marital infidelity, for example—shouldn't be dismissed or ignored, especially as it hurt other people in his life. But neither was this a retroactive disqualification, as his detractors would have it."

It is not my purpose here to defend or excuse King on any of the usual charges against him. I believe the historical record of his preaching, activism and eventual martyrdom already authenticate his spiritual mission. But regarding King's theology, Mark Noll said more in a sentence than I could say in an entire book when he wrote, "The religion of King and his associates was always more than just black evangelical revivalism, but it was never less."

Indeed, if I were a more daring polemicist, I might even be tempted to say that the theological expression of Martin Luther King Jr. has more in common with the work of later and contemporary African American *evangelical* activists and scholars than it does with that of many operating in more traditional black church contexts today. But that would probably get me in trouble.

"King is increasingly being used as a theological resource among evangelicals, especially among the younger generation," says New York Theological Seminary professor Peter Heltzel, who argues in his book *Jesus and Justice* that King's understanding of Christianity is best viewed "as a theology of the cross." After reading Heltzel's survey of the matter, it occurred to me that perhaps one of the reasons King's voice now resonates more clearly with evangelicals is because the Baptist preacher was speaking a more authentic version of their language all along. Heltzel believes that King "was calling white evangelicals back to the Gospels, back to their Savior, and back to the call to love thy neighbor." He adds, "Despite disagreement over whether King was an evangelical, it is clear that evangelicalism today is influenced by his legacy, justifying further study of how his life, faith, and theological vision fit within a history of evangelicalism."

It should be said that King certainly was a flawed man who was in regular need of God's grace, as we all are. But he also was a *chosen* man who was called to lead an unlikely movement, at a particular moment in time, against an immense system of social injustice. In an era when it was easy for good Christian people to be blinded to the obvious by both their cultural prejudice and human indifference, King saw things clearly. He knew he was on the right side of history. He understood that "the arc of the moral universe" always bends toward justice. This made his calling both easy and exceedingly difficult. And nowhere was this more evident than in Birmingham.

King's Epistle
for Today

So the question is not whether we will be extremists,
but what kind of extremists we will be.

Martin Luther King Jr.

At a black theology conference in August 1979, a decade after
Martin Luther King Jr.'s death, a group of African American theologians with all seriousness proposed that King's "Letter from Birmingham Jail" be added to the canon of New Testament Scripture
by the year 2000. This obviously didn't happen, but the gesture
reflects the high regard some feel for King's profound essay. Its list
of admirers is wide. South Africa's anti-apartheid movement adopted it as a rallying cry in the 1980s during its crusade to free
political prisoner Nelson Mandela; the late reggae star Bob Marley
kept a copy with him for good luck; it has been translated into
dozens of languages and used by nonviolent freedom movements
in Poland, East Germany, Argentina and Palestine.

Today in the United States, though the specific circumstances are
different, King's Birmingham epistle still provides insight and inspi-

ration on matters of racial justice, but also on issues as complex as income disparity, public education and immigration reform.

"Many of us who do speaking and training around the immigration issue are drawn to King's analysis in his letter of 'just' and 'unjust' law," says Joel Pérez, dean of students and community life at Seattle Pacific University. "As Christians addressing immigration, many of us think the fact that King's letter was written to clergy speaks volumes, especially for those of us in the church who are generally supportive of reform but don't want to risk speaking out for fear of rocking the boat." Pérez, who is Mexican American, says King challenges Christians on "the need to be active in working nonviolently to change law and policy that we know is not right in the eyes of God."

MAKING UP FOR LOST TIME

Carl Ruby, the former vice president of student life at Cedarville University in Ohio, shared with me the dramatic reorientation he experienced a few years ago after a visit to Birmingham. "I'm a lifelong Republican working at a conservative evangelical university," he told me, "so the political issues I'm concerned about are predetermined—low taxes, strong military, antiabortion." But something strange happened to him while visiting Sixteenth Street Baptist Church and touring the Birmingham Civil Rights Institute with a group of his students from Cedarville.

"I'm sure that at some point in my educational experience I must have been required to read 'Letter from a Birmingham Jail.' But back in high school I was a huge fan of Cliffs Notes and skimming instead of reading, so my awareness of the content of King's letter was vague at best." But as he stood in front of the Birmingham Jail exhibit at the Civil Rights Institute, surrounded by students, reading the excerpts from the letter on display next to the recreation of King's cell, Ruby says, "Martin Luther King quit being just a distant historical and political figure for me." He and his students were transported to 1963, and finally it all made sense. "Collectively, we experienced King for the first time as our brother in Christ, as he pleaded with fellow pastors to join his struggle for justice."

As he read more of the letter, Ruby was surprised at the depth of its theological reflection. "It wasn't filled with 'political' stuff; it was filled with 'Bible' stuff—things that resonated deeply with my evangelical faith—references to Shadrach, Meshach and Abednego, and to the apostle Paul, quotations from Augustine and Thomas Aquinas."

Most of all, Ruby was struck by how for so many years of his life, he simply could not grasp King's central message of justice and reconciliation. "King chided his fellow pastors for not recognizing that the lack of justice endured by their black brothers and sisters in Christ was a matter of spiritual and biblical significance," he says. "Well, I missed it, too. I grew up in a fundamentalist culture, and I never heard anything indicating that King was a good guy. For whatever reason, I couldn't see that King's 'inescapable network of mutuality' is a perfect description of the body of Christ. When one part hurts, we all hurt. Like Christ, we should be extremists for love, truth, and goodness."

Consequently, Ruby is now making up for lost time. During my visit to Cedarville's rural Ohio campus to speak at a King Day chapel, I was taken aback by the elaborate "Birmingham Jail" exhibit set up in the school's student commons, providing the campus community with the opportunity to experience King the way Ruby and his students had in Birmingham. It is a tribute to King that one hopes will continue after Ruby's exit. What's more, Ruby, the diehard Republican, has become a passionate advocate for a merciful and just Christian response to the immigration issue. When I asked him how his encounter with King led to this, he said, "I have grown up in churches that take great pride in 'preaching the Bible,' but I haven't heard a single sermon about my responsibility to care for the welfare of the strangers who have immigrated to the U.S., some whom live in my community. The church needs to be involved in this." Before Ruby left Cedarville in early 2013, he was instrumental in the school's hosting of the G92 Immigration Conference, which was billed as an "Evangelical Call for Bipartisan Immigration Reform." Ruby hopes it was just the first of an ongoing effort in the evangelical community.

Ruby says he doesn't want this generation of evangelicals to repeat the mistakes of the past. "I look back on the civil rights movement and wonder, 'How could most evangelicals have missed it? Why did they sit on the sidelines when the moral imperatives now seem so obvious?'"

WHERE DO WE GO FROM HERE?

If the Birmingham story does nothing else, it should inspire us—both as individuals and collective communities—to reexamine our relationship to justice. As Christians, have we allowed our cultural attachments and identities to overrule our ability to see truth? At the risk of becoming too formulaic or preachy, I'll wind down this book's extended reflection on Martin Luther King Jr., Birmingham and the church by sharing four concluding ideas that struck me as being essential to the success of the Birmingham revolution.

1. Know where your power comes from. The civil rights movement was grounded in the church and the holistic gospel of Jesus Christ. Popular history tends to remember only the secular portions of the boycotts, marches and famous speeches. But before Dr. King went to jail, he prayed. Before the children marched into the path of dogs and fire hoses, they sang hymns and prayed. "I Have a Dream" was one of the most effective political speeches ever delivered, but before that it was a sermon. Too many Christians in the public square today have allowed their politics to shape and define their faith. For Dr. King, it was always the other way around.

2. *Embrace your inner Shuttlesworth.* One of the most startling revelations that I had as I delved deeper into the Birmingham story is that the main protagonist of the event was not Martin King but Fred Shuttlesworth. Birmingham was Shuttlesworth's house; King was just visiting. But at the same time, Shuttlesworth understood that King had to take center stage in order for the campaign to succeed. He was a brash man, a fearless man, an uncompromising Christian man. He possessed tiny patience for people who were not ready to put their faith into action. Shuttlesworth, who died in 2011, lived boldly, resolutely and freely—even when Bull Connor told him he couldn't. At a 1998 conference honoring his life and work, he said, "If you wonder what made me act the fool, it was what Christ put in me, so you have to blame him." Shuttlesworth wasn't perfect, but he also wasn't afraid to use the gifts God gave him. What's more, he knew when to get out of the way and allow God to work through someone else.

3. *"Let no man despise your youth."* Children and teenagers were crucial to the success of the Birmingham campaign. It certainly was radical for the movement to place kids right in the middle of what proved to be a war zone. Yet the leaders' faith in their young people, and the young people's exuberant faith in a higher ideal, turned out to be the decisive factor in the Birmingham victory. If we allow them, young people will lead. So trust them, train them and empower them. Show them how to rely on God for themselves. Then give them a worthy mission that means something.

4. *Live your letter.* The initial draft of "Letter from Birmingham Jail"—with its riffs on Socrates, Aquinas, Thomas Jefferson, Frederick Douglass and Martin Buber (not to mention Jesus and Paul)—was written extemporaneously, drawn from King's photographic memory and exegetical brilliance. King was a well-read man who possessed a flair for "absorbing and synthesizing" the

great ideas of great thinkers. Though he has been rightly criticized for his academic shortcuts in grad school, "Letter from Birmingham Jail" makes it resplendently clear that he was no intellectual fraud. Not only could King wrestle with Western civilization's big concepts of religion, politics and philosophy, he could do it while under siege by a vicious racist. As one biographer put it, "King's exegesis from Birmingham's jail . . . became his true doctoral thesis." But the words that came spilling out of King were not just abstract blather that he used to sound important (though he certainly loved to turn a good phrase). Rather, King's words in the Birmingham letter represented a transcription of his life message— the narrative that he not only *spoke* but was attempting to *live*. It was a narrative of peace, reconciliation and justice. Through prayer, study and reflection, King was able to tell his story compellingly when the time arrived because his letter was his life.

TRUTH MARCHES ON

The great Russian novelist Leo Tolstoy, who like King also struggled with bouts of guilt and self-flagellation, once said: "It is easier to write ten volumes of philosophy than to put a single precept into practice." However, "Letter from Birmingham Jail" proves that Martin Luther King Jr. was someone able to do both philosophy and practice extremely well, though not without great struggle and strain.

And during a singular period in 1963, all that he knew about the nature of justice, all that he wanted to make known about the truth of the gospel, and all that he was compelled to be as an "extremist" for Christ came spilling out onto paper to form his most important written work. In Birmingham, King was able to both write and practice a holistic vision of what it means to be a Christian in a broken and unjust world. Fifty years later we're still reading and being transformed by his letter. It may not be canon, but it is truth.

"Black Tuesday, May 7, 1963," demonstration; photograph is from the Birmingham Police Department Surveillence Files

(Used by permission of Birmingham, Alabama, Public Library Archives.)

Demonstration of Fifth Avenue North; looking toward Kelly Ingram Park. In the park, water spraying from at least two fire hoses can be seen.

(Used by permission of Birmingham, Alabama, Public Library Archives.)

ACKNOWLEDGMENTS

WRITING ANY BOOK is a humbling experience. Having the nerve to write a book about Martin Luther King Jr. is downright ridiculous. One has to first confront the question, *Is another King book really necessary?* In the grand scheme of things, probably not. For me, however, it became a curiosity and then an obsession. But first it was a graduation requirement for my master's degree. Which leads me to the first of my acknowledgments.

Back in 2010 I went back to college to earn my master's degree in philosophy of history at Olivet Nazarene University. I started off as the third oldest student in my cohort, but by the end of the two-year program I was the forty-something elder among a class of sharp twenty-something scholars who were much smarter than I. I learned a lot from each of them. I'm especially grateful to Professors William Dean and David Van Heemst for their leadership and instruction. When I was debating entering the program, Dr. Dean met me at a McDonald's one morning to discuss the prospect with me. His wisdom and kind spirit eventually sold me on signing up. And Dr. Van Heemst, something of a rock star political scientist on the Olivet campus, was the first to suggest that I consider homing in on King's "Letter from Birmingham Jail" as the subject for my master's thesis. His insight and encouragement nudged me down the path that would lead to this book. In addition, Curt Rice, Gary Hyde, Joan Dean and Brian Woodworth each played key roles in my Olivet journey.

No one can write a book about MLK, Birmingham and the civil rights movement without encountering and relying on a slew of historians, journalists and authors who did it first. Most of them are listed in my end notes and bibliography, but several stand out for special mention: Lewis Baldwin, Taylor Branch, Stewart Burns, Clayborne Carson, Glenn T. Eskew, David J. Garrow, Vincent Harding, Richard Lischer, Andrew Manis, Diane McWhorter and Stephen B. Oates.

This book's coverage of the eight Birmingham clergymen who inspired King's "Letter" would have been impossible without the seminal scholarship found in S. Jonathan Bass's *Blessed Are the Peacemakers*. Bass's tome is currently the most exhaustive work on the lives and ministries of the eight men whose legacies are forever tied to King's. As a secondhand historian I'm grateful for Bass's unique contribution.

I'm also thankful for the personal friendship, encouragement, and professional assistance of numerous men and women: Joel Kneedler, Julie J. Park, Alvin Sanders, Randy Woodley, Curtiss Paul DeYoung, Joel Pérez, Debra Dean Murphy, Jennifer Parker, Jerald January, Alison Burkhardt, William Pannell, Kevin Moore, Michael Wesley, Tracy Hipps, Janice Kelsey, Edward J. Blum, Pastor John Byrd, Carl Ruby, Lynn McCain, Brenda Salter McNeil, Carl Jeffrey Wright, Melvin Banks, Jennifer Schuchmann, Michael O. Emerson, Mickey Maudlin and Christine Scheller. And a huge thanks to all the folks who were kind enough to provide endorsement blurbs for this book.

Courtney Chartier, assistant head of the Archives Research Center at the Atlanta University Center's Robert W. Woodruff Library, was helpful in guiding me through the Center's King Collection and answering my many questions. Don Veasey and Jim Baggett at the Birmingham Public Library were also quick to respond to my inquiries about their city's history. Lynn Hammerlund and the other librarians at my alma mater Judson University provided a quiet place for me to work at the Benjamin P. Browne Library during a pivotal time in my writing of this book.

I am grateful to Bob Fryling and InterVarsity Press for once again taking a chance on me as an author. Cindy Bunch is the smartest, toughest and most understanding editor anyone could hope for. I'm also appreciative of the passionate commitment of Jeff Crosby, as well as the diligent work of Ben McCoy, Krista Carnet, Adrianna Wright, Ellen Hsu, Rachel Willoughby, Alisse Wissman, Deborah Gonzalez, Jon Boyd and Andrew Bronson.

I am forever thankful for the legacy of my late parents Ed and Florence Gilbreath, without whom I obviously would not be here today. They were the first to teach me about Martin Luther King Jr. and the value of love, justice and freedom.

I owe so much to my wife, Dana, and children, DeMara and Daniel, who learned to live with my crankiness and virtual absences during the long months of my graduate program and the writing of this book. Thanks for the unconditional love.

Finally, I would be remiss if I didn't acknowledge the ministry, work and sacrifice of all the men, women and children who gave so much so that we could be a better nation today. Martin Luther King Jr. and Fred Shuttlesworth get the starring roles in this book, but there are countless others, living and deceased, who deserve our gratitude and admiration.

Above all, I give thanks to God for the privilege of being able to write words for a living. May they always be used to tell his story.

Notes

OPENING EPIGRAPH

page 8   James Baldwin and Reinhold Niebuhr quotes are from *The Meaning of the Birmingham Tragedy*, September 22, 1963, a New York City television special moderated by Rev. Thomas Kilgore; audio posted at the *On Being with Krista Tippett* website, www.onbeing.org/program/moral-man-and-immoral-society-rediscovering-reinhold-niebuhr/feature/sermons-and-lectures#main_content.

PROLOGUE

page 9   Luther quote: Heiko Oberman, *Luther: Man Between God and the Devil* (New Haven, CT.: Yale University Press, 1989), p. 39; King quote: "Letter from Birmingham Jail," *Martin Luther King, Jr., and the Global Freedom Struggle,* http://mlk-kpp01.stanford.edu/index.php/encyclopedia/documentsentry/annotated_letter_from_birmingham.

page 9   Martin Luther was on a mission: See Diarmaid MacCulloch, *The Reformation: A History* (New York: Viking, 2003), pp. 119-20. One of many helpful histories of the Reformation and Luther's life.

page 10   We hold these truths: "Declaration of Independence," 1776, www.ushistory.org/declaration/document.

page 11   "The discovery of personal whiteness": W. E. B. Du Bois, "The Souls of White Folk," *Independent*, August 18, 1910, p. 339. This essay was republished in a revised form in W. E. B. Du Bois, *Darkwater* (New York: Harcourt, Brace & Howe, 1920).

page 12   "Our nation was born in genocide": Martin Luther King Jr., *Why We Can't Wait* (New York: New American Library, 1964), pp. 130-31.

page 15   "But the end is reconciliation": Martin Luther King Jr., *The Papers of Martin Luther King, Jr.,* ed. Clayborne Carson et al. (Berkeley: University of California Press, 1997), 3:458.

page 15   "every medium of mutual interest": Harrison E. Salisbury, "Fear and Hatred Grip Birmingham, April 1960," in *Reporting Civil Rights,* part 1, *American Journalism 1941-1963,* ed. Clayborne Carson et al. (New York: Literary Classics, 2003), p. 447-52.

page 15   "My Dear Fellow Clergymen": Throughout the book, I reference the version of "Letter from Birmingham Jail" found at the Stanford University MLK Research and Education Institute website, *Martin Luther King, Jr., and the Global Freedom Struggle,* http://mlk-kpp01.stanford.edu/index.php/encyclopedia/documentsentry/annotated_letter_from_birmingham.

page 16   As one biographer noted: Marshall Frady, *Martin Luther King, Jr.: A Life* (New York: Penguin, 2006), pp. 107-8.

page 16   "Dr. King wanted all Christians to embrace": Alvin Sanders, email interview with the author, January 22, 2013.

page 17   "King's letter reads like a kick in the stomach": Julie J. Park, email interview with the author, January 5, 2013.

CHAPTER 1: BIRMINGHAM BEGINS

page 19   From 1910 to 1970: Nicholas Lemann, *The Promised Land: The Great Black Migration and How It Changed America* (New York: Knopf, 1991), pp. 6-7.

page 19   "unrecognized immigration": Isabel Wilkerson, *The Warmth of Other Suns: The Epic Story of America's Great Migration* (New York: Random House, 2010), p. 536.

page 19   "Some came straight from the field": Ibid., p. 9.

page 21   Birmingham was seen as the Promised Land: See Glenn T. Eskew, *But for Birmingham: The Local and National Movements in the Civil Rights Struggle* (Chapel Hill: University of North Carolina Press, 1997); and Andrew M. Manis, *A Fire You Can't Put Out: The Civil Rights Life of Birmingham's Reverend Fred Shuttlesworth* (Tuscaloosa: University of Alabama Press, 1999).

page 21   Newly elected Warren G. Harding: David Keene, "A Second Look at Harding," *The Hill,* November 23, 2009, http://thehill

.com/opinion/columnists/david-keene/69203-a-second-look-at-harding.

page 22   Birmingham as the South's largest segregated city: Charles E. Cobb Jr., *On the Road to Freedom: A Guided Tour of the Civil Rights Trail* (Chapel Hill, NC: Algonquin Books, 2007), pp. 249-58.

page 22   "blood would flow in the streets first": Attributed to Georgia governor George Talmadge and others in "What Negroes Want Now," Walter White, interview by *U.S. News & World Report*, May 28, 1954, www.crmvet.org/info/54_naacp_walter_white.pdf.

page 22   The city's legendary public safety commissioner: See Larry Dane Brimner, *Black & White: The Confrontation Between Fred L. Shuttlesworth and Eugene "Bull" Connor* (Honesdale, PA: Calkins Creek, 2011).

page 23   "It was a turbulent period of time": Michael W. Wesley, telephone interview with the author, February 4, 2013.

page 23   Till was visiting relatives: Brimner, *Black & White*, p. 21.

page 23   "Churches helped black migrants adjust": Wilson Fallin Jr., "Rock Solid Faith: African American Church Life and Culture in 1956 Birmingham," in *Birmingham's Revolutionary: The Reverend Fred Shuttlesworth and the Alabama Christian Movement for Human Rights*, ed. Marjorie L. White and Andrew M. Manis (Macon, GA: Mercer University Press, 2000), pp. 8-11.

page 24   National Association for the Advancement of Colored People: Adam Fairclough, *Better Day Coming: Blacks and Equality, 1890-2000* (New York: Penguin, 2001), pp. 67-70.

pages 24-25 NAACP's temporary expulsion from Alabama: Diane Mc-Whorter, *Carry Me Home: Birmingham, Alabama—The Climatic Battle of the Civil Rights Revolution* (New York: Simon & Schuster, 2001), pp. 107-8.

page 25   "I confess to being a great criminal": Fred Shuttlesworth, quoted in Fallin, *Birmingham's Revolutionary*, p. 75.

page 25   Born March 18, 1922, to unmarried parents: Manis, *A Fire You Can't Put Out*, pp. 10-34.

page 25   "I believed in them": Fred Shuttlesworth, quoted in Adam

Fairclough, *Teaching Equality: Black Schools in the Age of Jim Crow* (Athens: University of Georgia Press, 2001), p. 42.

page 25   Working variously as a truck driver and substitute teacher: Taylor Branch, *Parting the Waters: America in the King Years, 1954-1963* (New York: Simon & Schuster, 1988), p. 87.

page 26   In 1953 he accepted the full-time pastorate: Manis, *A Fire You Can't Put Out*, p. 69.

page 26   Earned a reputation as his city's most outspoken civil rights warrior: Ibid., pp. 72-90.

page 26   Shores's legal efforts: Branch, *Parting the Waters*, pp. 868, 888.

page 27   On a warm June night in 1956: Brimner, *Black & White*, pp. 25-26.

page 27   White leaders could not ban "the determination in people's minds and hearts": Fred Shuttlesworth interview, *Eyes on the Prize: America's Civil Rights Years (1954-1965)*. November 7, 1985, Washington University Libraries, Film and Media Archive, http://digital.wustl.edu/e/eop/eopweb/shu0015.0366.096revfredshuttlesworth.html.

page 27   seven-point Declaration of Principles: Manis, *A Fire You Can't Put Out*, pp. 96-97.

page 27   Shuttlesworth as president of ACMHR,: Ibid., pp. 94, 114-16.

page 27   "Somebody has to go to jail": Shuttlesworth interview, *Eyes on the Prize*.

page 27   Federal courts ruled in favor of the ACMHR: "Fred Shuttlesworth," Spartacus Educational, www.spartacus.schoolnet.co.uk/USAshutterworth.htm.

page 28   Shuttlesworth became a prime target of Bull Connor: Howell Raines, *My Soul Is Rested: The Story of the Civil Rights Movement in the Deep South* (New York: Penguin, 1983), pp. 154-55.

page 28   "Shuttlesworth was a Daniel in his own right": Andrew M. Manis, "A Fire You Can't Put Out: The Meanings of Fred Shuttlesworth and His Movement," in *Birmingham's Revolutionary*, p. 59.

page 29   "the Wild Man from Birmingham": McWhorter, *Carry Me Home*, pp. 21-22.

page 29   "like getting religion again": Shuttlesworth interview, *Eyes on the Prize*.

page 29   network of African American pastors: Fallin, in "Rock Solid Faith," pp. 9-11.

page 29   Shuttlesworth at Montgomery's Holt Street Baptist Church: Shuttlesworth interview, *Eyes on the Prize*.

CHAPTER 2: THE MAKING OF MARTIN

page 32   I strained to imagine the *real* King: David J. Garrow, *Bearing the Cross: Martin Luther King, Jr. and the Southern Christian Leadership Conference* (London: Vintage, 1986), pp. 34-35.

page 32   "The history of the world is but": Thomas Carlyle, *On Heroes and Hero Worship and the Heroic in History* (1840), Project Gutenberg, www.gutenberg.org/files/1091/1091-h/1091-h.htm.

page 33   He was born Michael Luther King Jr.: Clayborne Carson, ed., *The Autobiography of Martin Luther King, Jr.* (New York: Warner Books 1998).

page 33   Name change to Martin Luther King: Taylor Branch, *Parting the Waters: America in the King Years, 1954-1963* (New York: Simon & Schuster, 1988), p. 44.

page 33   Williams promoted "a strategy that combined elements": Rufus Burrow Jr., *Martin Luther King Jr. for Armchair Theologians* (Louisville: Westminster John Knox Press, 2009), p. 32.

page 33   He also prayed—and, indeed, expected: Harvard Sitkoff, *King: Pilgrimage to the Mountaintop* (New York: Hill & Wang, 2008), p. 3.

page 33   Daddy King mentored by his father-in-law: Burrow, *Martin Luther King Jr. for Armchair Theologians*, p. 35.

page 33   the King home was warm and loving: Garrow, *Bearing the Cross*, p. 33.

page 34   "Not wealthy really": David Halberstam, "The Second Coming of Martin Luther King," in *Reporting Civil Rights*, part 2, *American Journalism 1963-1973*, ed. Clayborne Carson et al. (New York: Literary Classics, 2003), p. 574.

page 34   "That's a boy. I'm a man": Martin Luther King Jr., *The Autobiography of Martin Luther King, Jr.*, ed. Clayborne Carson (New York: Warner Books 1998), pp. 7-8.

page 35   "You are that little nigger": Ibid., pp. 7-8.

page 35   "I should not hate the white man": Ibid., pp. 6-7.

page 35   Raised under the religious pieties: Lewis V. Baldwin, *There Is a Balm in Gilead: The Cultural Roots of Martin Luther King Jr.* (Minneapolis: Augsburg Fortress Press, 1991), pp. 160-61.

page 35   "They taught the Bible at Ebenezer Baptist Church": Edward Gilbreath, "Catching Up with a Dream," *Christianity Today*, March 2, 1998, jciknccceverddgcwww.ctlibrary.com/ct/1998/march2/8t3020.html.

page 35   he had developed a supercilious distaste: Halberstam, "The Second Coming of Martin Luther King," p. 574.

pages 35-36 Though both his grandfather and father had determined: Marshall Frady, *Martin Luther King, Jr.: A Life* (New York: Penguin, 2006), p.16.

page 36   only an average student: Garrow, *Bearing the Cross*, p. 37.

page 36   "He was so young looking": Coretta Scott King, quoted in *New Time, New Voice*, a video at the Martin Luther King Jr. National Historic Site Visitors Center, Atlanta, Georgia, viewed on April 3, 2012.

pages 36-37 He earned a reputation as a ladies' man: Garrow, *Bearing the Cross*, p. 36.

page 37   "we had many white persons as allies": King, *Autobiography*, p. 14.

page 37   "Both were ministers, both deeply religious": Ibid., p.16.

page 37   King was intrigued by the concept of refusing cooperation: Ibid., p. 14.

page 38   not an emotional, Damascus Road-type decision: Frady, *Martin Luther King, Jr.*, p. 18.

page 38   "the effects of the noble moral and ethical ideals": King, *Autobiography*, p. 16.

page 38   He entered Crozer: Ibid., p. 17-18.

page 38   As a PhD student in systematic theology: Ibid., p. 32.

pages 38-39 Blend of African-Baptist and liberal theological traditions: Richard Lischer, *The Preacher King: Martin Luther King Jr. and the Word That Moved America* (New York: Oxford University Press, 1995), p. 5.

page 39   "We said that Daddy King had raised Martin right": Philip Yancey, *Soul Survivor: How My Faith Survived the Church* (New York: Doubleday, 2001), p. 17.

page 39   segregation prevented attendance at more conservative Christian schools: Garrow, *Bearing the Cross*, pp. 42-44.

page 39   glaring examples of derivative material and even plagiarism: MLK Research and Education Institute, "Dissertation of Martin Luther King, Jr." (1955), Martin Luther King, Jr., and the Global Freedom Struggle, http://mlk-kpp01.stanford.edu/index.php/encyclopedia/encyclopedia/enc_dissertation_of_martin_luther_king_jr_1955.

page 39   an overreliance on the oral tradition: Curtiss Paul DeYoung, *Living Faith: How Faith Inspires Social Justice* (Minneapolis: Fortress Press, 2007), pp. 130-31.

pages 39-40   "carelessness and lapses in academic honesty": Lischer, *Preacher King*, p. 63.

page 40   "a moral obligation to return to the South": King, *Autobiography*, p. 44.

page 40   "our greatest service could be rendered in our native South": Ibid., p. 44.

page 41   "The Three Dimensions of a Complete Life": Ibid., p. 43.

page 41   Dexter's worshipers were impressed: Garrow, *Bearing the Cross*, pp. 48-49.

CHAPTER 3: MONTGOMERY MIRACLE

page 46   Dexter was a prestigious African American congregation: David J. Garrow, *Bearing the Cross: Martin Luther King, Jr. and the Southern Christian Leadership Conference* (London: Vintage, 1986), p. 48.

page 47   "The doctrine of white supremacy cast a pall": Troy Jackson, *Becoming King: Martin Luther King Jr. and the Making of a National Leader* (Lexington: University Press of Kentucky, 2008), p. 83.

page 47   Parks's arrest as a rallying point: Taylor Branch, *Parting the Waters: America in the King Years, 1954-1963* (New York: Simon & Schuster, 1988), pp. 136-37.

page 48   five thousand people filled the sanctuary: Garrow, *Bearing the Cross*, p. 23.

page 48   Montgomery campaign continued 381 days: "Montgomery Bus Boycott (1955-1956)," Martin Luther King, Jr., and the Global Freedom Struggle, http://mlk-kpp01.stanford.edu/

index.php/encyclopedia/encyclopedia/enc_montgomery_
bus_boycott_1955_1956.

page 48   Billy Graham invited King to lead prayer: Howard O. Jones
             with Edward Gilbreath, *Gospel Trailblazer: An African-
             American Preacher's Historic Journey Across Racial Lines*
             (Chicago: Moody Press, 2003), p. 144.

page 49   "My family and I had to get involved": Robert Graetz, quoted
             in Edward Gilbreath, "Catching Up with a Dream," *Christi-
             anity Today*, March 2, 1998, www.ctlibrary.com/ct/1998/
             march2/8t3020.html. Original telephone interview, December
             15, 1997.

page 49   King also thought highly of Graetz: Martin Luther King Jr.,
             Stride Toward Freedom, quoted in *A Testament of Hope: The Es-
             sential Writings and Speeches of Martin Luther King, Jr.*, ed.
             James M. Washington (San Francisco: HarperSanFrancisco,
             1986), p. 440.

page 50   Azbell was taken aback by the uprising: Troy Jackson, *Be-
             coming King: Martin Luther King Jr. and the Making of a Na-
             tional Leader* (Lexington: University Press of Kentucky,
             2008), p. 122.td

page 51   King was concerned about Daddy King: Martin Luther King
             Jr., *The Autobiography of Martin Luther King, Jr.*, ed. Clayborne
             Carson (New York: Warner Books 1998), p. 76.

page 51   A turning point came in January 1956: Ibid., pp. 76-78.

page 52   this supernatural event further confirmed: Lewis V. Baldwin,
             *Never to Leave Us Alone: The Prayer Life of Martin Luther King
             Jr.* (Minneapolis: Fortress Press, 2010), pp. 69-70.

page 52   test drive the ideas of nonviolent resistance: Lewis V.
             Baldwin, *There Is a Balm in Gilead: The Cultural Roots of
             Martin Luther King Jr.* (Minneapolis: Augsburg Fortress
             Press, 1991), p. 65.

page 52   Montgomery "as an act of massive noncooperation": King,
             Autobiography, p. 54.

page 52   "drive against injustice can bring great tangible gains": King,
             quoted in Washington, ed., *A Testament of Hope*, p. xix.

pages 52-53 formation of the Southern Christian Leadership Conference:
             Branch, *Parting the Waters*, pp. 198-99.

page 53   "Dr. King was chosen because he . . . was qualified": Fred
             Shuttlesworth interview, *Eyes on the Prize: America's Civil
             Rights Years (1954-1965)*. November 7, 1985, Washington
             University Libraries, Film and Media Archive, http://digital
             .wustl.edu/e/eop/eopweb/shu0015.0366.096revfredshuttles
             worth.html.

CHAPTER 4: THE ROAD TO REVOLUTION

page 54   "I think the theme Dr. King was developing": Randy Woodley,
             email interview with the author, January 7, 2013.

page 54   "the spirituality of risk and doing": Ibid.

page 56   "History has thrust something upon me": Martin Luther King
             Jr., quoted in Martin Frady, *Martin Luther King, Jr.: A Life*
             (New York: Penguin, 2006), p. 53.

page 56   "The average man reaches this point": Martin Luther King Jr.,
             The Autobiography of Martin Luther King, Jr., ed. Clayborne
             Carson (New York: Warner Books 1998), p. 106.

page 56   "a modern Moses": Ira Peck, *The Life and Words of Martin
             Luther King, Jr.* (New York: Scholastic, 1968), p. 46.

page 56   "the key to the whole solution": Frady, *Martin Luther King, Jr.*,
             p. 54.

page 56   SCLC helped mobilize a prayer pilgrimage: King, *Autobiog-
             raphy*, p. 108.

page 57   King's relationship with his father: Frady, *Martin Luther King,
             Jr.*, p. 54.

page 57   King remained largely on the sidelines: Harvard Sitkoff, *King:
             Pilgrimage to the Mountaintop* (New York: Hill & Wang,
             2008), pp. 68-69.

page 58   "After we had started sitting in": Diane Nash, quoted in Henry
             Hampton and Steve Foyer, *Voices of Freedom: An Oral History
             of the Civil Rights Movement from the 1950s Through the 1980s*
             (New York: Bantam Books, 1990), p. 58.

page 58   "When it was time to go to jail": Ibid., p. 59.

page 58   Student Nonviolent Coordinating Committee: Sitkoff, *King*,
             p. 70.

page 58   King as "de Lawd": Diane McWhorter, *Carry Me Home: Bir-
             mingham, Alabama—The Climatic Battle of the Civil Rights*

Revolution (New York: Simon & Schuster, 2001), p. 238.

page 59   King's incarceration made national headlines: Ira Peck, *The Life and Words of Martin Luther King, Jr.* (New York: Scholastic, 1968), p. 50.

page 59   In 1961 the Freedom Rides: Hampton and Fayer, *Voices of Freedom*, p. 74.

page 60   The Freedom Riders elicited violent reactions: Peck, *Life and Words of Martin Luther King, Jr.*, pp. 50-51.

page 60   "the quiet courage of dying for a cause": Larry A. Still, "A Bus Ride Through Mississippi," *Ebony*, August 1961, p. 22.

page 61   At the center of the chaos: Andrew M. Manis, *A Fire You Can't Put Out: The Civil Rights Life of Birmingham's Reverend Fred Shuttlesworth* (Tuscaloosa: University of Alabama Press, 1999), pp. 263-66.

page 61   King would encounter his first formidable challenge: See Charles E. Cobb Jr., *On the Road to Freedom: A Guided Tour of the Civil Rights Trail* (Chapel Hill, NC: Algonquin Books, 2008), pp. 179-90.

page 62   "We're going to out-nonviolent them": Laurie Pritchett, quoted in Hampton and Fayer, *Voices of Freedom*, p. 106.

page 62   The Albany authorities kept pressing: Peck, *Life and Words of Martin Luther King, Jr.*, p. 53.

page 62   "We lost an initiative that we never regained": King, *Autobiography*, p. 167.

CHAPTER 5: AS BIRMINGHAM GOES

page 63   1961 CBS documentary *Who Speaks for Birmingham?*: Howard K. Smith, "Who Speaks for Birmingham?" *CBS Reports*, May 18, 1961.

page 63   Pulitzer Prize-winning journalist Harrison Salisbury: Diane McWhorter, *Carry Me Home: Birmingham, Alabama—The Climatic Battle of the Civil Rights Revolution* (New York: Simon & Schuster, 2001), pp. 157-59.

page 64   40 percent of Birmingham's residents were African American: Henry Hampton and Steve Fayer, *Voices of Freedom: An Oral History of the Civil Rights Movement from the 1950s Through the 1980s* (New York: Bantam Books, 1990), p. 124.

page 65 "bottled in the slums": Glenn T. Eskew, *But for Birmingham: The Local and National Movements in the Civil Rights Struggle* (Chapel Hill: University of North Carolina Press, 1997), p. 63.

page 65 conservative businessman Arthur "A. G." Gaston: Mc-Whorter, *Carry Me Home*, pp. 262-63.

page 65 Gaston funded Shuttlesworth: Hampton and Fayer, *Voices of Freedom*, p. 129.

page 65 attacks against the Freedom Riders were an atrocity: Ibid., p. 124.

page 66 many pronounced nonviolent resistance "a dead issue": Martin Luther King Jr., *The Autobiography of Martin Luther King, Jr.*, ed. Clayborne Carson (New York: Warner Books 1998), p. 168.

page 66 Shuttlesworth leaves Birmingham's Bethel Baptist Church: Andrew M. Manis, *A Fire You Can't Put Out: The Civil Rights Life of Birmingham's Reverend Fred Shuttlesworth* (Tuscaloosa: University of Alabama Press, 1999), pp. 281-82.

page 67 Shuttlesworth urges a campaign in Birmingham: Ibid., p. 221.

page 67 Biographer Andrew Manis recounts: Ibid., pp. 221-222.

page 67 "King's image was slightly on the wane": Fred Shuttlesworth, quoted in Hampton and Fayer, *Voices of Freedom*, pp. 124-25.

page 68 confront segregation "with our bodies and souls": Ira Peck, *The Life and Words of Martin Luther King, Jr.* (New York: Scholastic, 1968), p. 53.

page 68 "After Albany, Dr. King decided": Wyatt Tee Walker, quoted in Hampton and Fayer, *Voices of Freedom*, p. 125.

page 68 direct aim at Birmingham's economic system: Peck, *Life and Words of Martin Luther King, Jr.*, p. 54.

pages 68-69 twenty-four college students staged sit-ins: Charles E. Cobb Jr., *On the Road to Freedom: A Guided Tour of the Civil Rights Trail* (Chapel Hill, NC: Algonquin Books, 2008), pp. 251-52.

page 69 Initially, Bull Connor exercised restraint: Peck, *Life and Words of Martin Luther King, Jr.,* p. 55.

page 69 King was caught at an impasse: Harvard Sitkoff, *King: Pilgrimage to the Mountaintop* (New York: Hill & Wang, 2008), pp. 92-94.

page 70 "a sense of doom began to pervade the room": King, *Autobiography*, p. 182.

page 70   "standing at the center of all that my life": Ibid., pp. 182-83.
page 70   King returned to his colleagues in room 30: Sitkoff, *King*, p. 94.
page 70   "we all linked hands involuntarily": King, *Autobiography*, p. 183.
page 71   King and Abernathy set out on their fateful march: Martin
              Frady, *Martin Luther King, Jr.: A Life* (New York: Penguin,
              2006), pp. 105-6.

CHAPTER 6: EIGHT WHITE PREACHERS,
OR WITH FRIENDS LIKE THESE

page 72   "We do not believe that these days of new hope": "Good Friday
              Statement by Eight Alabama Clergymen," Priests for Life, April
              12, 1963, www.priestsforlife.org/articles/kingltroriginal.htm.
page 73   "Unfortunately, the president of the convention": Dwight
              McKissic, quoted in Christine A. Scheller, "Rev. Fred Luter
              Elected to SBC Presidency," UrbanFaith.com, June 19, 2012,
              www.urbanfaith.com/2012/06/rev-fred-luter-elected-to-sbc-
              presidency.html.
page 74   In my 2006 book *Reconciliation Blues*: See Ed Gilbreath,
              "When Blacks Quit Evangelical Institutions," *Reconciliation
              Blues: A Black Evangelical's Inside View of White Christianity*
              (Downers Grove, IL, 2006), pp. 84-99.
page 74   One of those leaders was Rev. Jerald January: In *Reconciliation
              Blues* I was asked to give Jerald a pseudonym: "Darrell Davis."
              That restriction has since been dropped.
page 77   The local *Birmingham News*: S. Jonathan Bass, *Blessed Are the
              Peacemakers: Martin Luther King Jr., Eight White Religious
              Leaders, and the "Letter from Birmingham Jail"* (Baton Rouge:
              Louisiana State University Press, 2001), p. 103.
page 77   *Time* criticized King's campaign: Harvard Sitkoff, *King: Pil-
              grimage to the Mountaintop* (New York: Hill & Wang, 2008),
              p. 95.
page 77   *Washington Post* described King's demonstrations: Bass,
              Blessed Are the Peacemakers, p. 105.
page 77   the *Post* and *New York Times* opined: Diane McWhorter, *Carry
              Me Home: Birmingham, Alabama—The Climatic Battle of the
              Civil Rights Revolution* (New York: Simon & Schuster, 2001),
              pp. 352-53.

page 77   "it was ridiculous to speak of timing": Martin Luther King Jr.,
           Why We Can't Wait, quoted in James M. Washington, ed., *A
           Testament of Hope: The Essential Writings and Speeches of
           Martin Luther King* (San Francisco: HarperSanFrancisco,
           1986), p. 539.

page 78   Billy Graham suggested that his "good personal friend":
           Nancy Gibbs and Michael Duffy, *The Preacher and the Presi-
           dents: Billy Graham in the White House* (New York: Center
           Street, 2007), p. 111.

page 78   "bad timing" became "ghosts haunting": King, quoted in
           Washington, ed., *A Testament of Hope*, p. 539.

page 78   King's presence as an interloping agitator: David J. Garrow,
           *Bearing the Cross: Martin Luther King, Jr. and the Southern
           Christian Leadership Conference* (London: Vintage, 1986), p. 240.

page 78   Jackson strongly opposed racial segregation: Bass, *Blessed Are
           the Peacemakers*, p. 105.

page 79   "My place on the chamber": A. G. Gaston, quoted in Henry
           Hampton and Steve Fayer, *Voices of Freedom: An Oral History
           of the Civil Rights Movement from the 1950s Through the 1980s*
           (New York: Bantam Books, 1990), p. 129.

page 79   the inauguration of Governor George Wallace: Bass, *Blessed
           Are the Peacemakers*, pp. 18-20.

page 80   death threats and charges of "communists": Ibid., pp. 24-25.

page 80   "We the undersigned clergymen": See Bass, *Blessed Are the
           Peacemakers*, pp. 235-36, and "The Following Is the Public
           Statement Directed to Martin Luther King, Jr., by Eight Al-
           abama Clergymen," Priests for Life, www.priestsforlife.org/
           articles/kingltroriginal.htm.

page 83   "SCLC preachers wanted extensive press coverage": Bass,
           Blessed Are the Peacemakers, p. 24.

page 84   Birmingham Eight were more than symbols: Ibid., pp. 5-6.

page 84   different points on the "moderate" spectrum: Ibid., pp. 22-23.

page 84   Bishop Durick and Rabbi Grafman: Ibid., pp. 55, 60-61.

page 85   The über-gradualists: Ibid., pp. 44-45.

page 85   The meta-moderates: Ibid., pp. 46-48.

page 86   The reluctant radicals: Ibid., p. 86.

CHAPTER 7: AN ANGRY DR. KING

page 89   a man gets tired of wearing that façade: See Paul Laurence
              Dunbar, "We Wear the Mask," in *The Life and Works of Paul
              Laurence Dunbar* (Nashville: Winston-Derek, 1992), p. 184.

page 89   the phenomenon scholars call "everyday racism": "Hiding
              Emotions May Exacerbate Depression Among Black Men
              Who Confront Racial Discrimination," *University of North
              Carolina at Chapel Hill News*, March 14, 2012, http://uncnews
              .unc.edu/content/view/5164/107.

page 90   "anti-anti-racists": Michelle Goldberg, "Why Conservatives
              Are Smearing Trayvon Martin's Reputation," *Daily Beast*,
              March 27, 2012, www.thedailybeast.com/articles/2012/03/26/
              why-conservatives-are-smearing-trayvon-martin-s-reputation
              .html.

page 92   King recalled a particularly painful incident: Martin Luther
              King Jr., *Playboy* interview, January 1965, cited in James M.
              Washington, ed., *A Testament of Hope: The Essential Writings
              and Speeches of Martin Luther King* (San Francisco: Harper-
              SanFrancisco, 1986), pp. 342-43.

page 92   "strong capacity to experience anger": Hitendra Wadhwa, "The
              Wrath of a Great Leader," *Inc.*, January 15, 2012, www.inc.com/
              hitendra-wadhwa/great-leadership-how-martin-luther-king-jr-
              wrestled-with-anger.html.

pages 93-94 "Martin always felt that anger": Harry Belafonte, quoted in
              Stephen B. Oates, *Let the Trumpet Sound: The Life of Martin
              Luther King, Jr.* (New York: Harper & Row, 1982), p. 274.

page 93   At the zenith of his career: King, quoted in Washington, ed.,
              Testament of Hope, p. 360.

page 93   "Santa Claus-ification of Martin Luther King": Cornel West,
              "Stop the 'Santa Claus-ification' of Martin Luther King,"
              Rolling Out, January 18, 2010, http://rollingout.com/enter-
              tainment/stop-the-santa-claus-ification-of-martin-luther-
              king-pleads-dr-cornel-west.

page 94   "We have transformed King": Timothy B. Tyson, *Blood Done
              Sign My Name: A True Story* (New York: Three Rivers Press,
              2004), p. 107.

page 94   King sat alone in the city jail: King, quoted in Washington, ed., *Testament of Hope*, p. 544.

page 94   King was allowed no phone calls: Martin Luther King Jr., *The Autobiography of Martin Luther King, Jr.*, ed. Clayborne Carson (New York: Warner Books 1998), p. 184.

page 95   "think long thoughts and pray long prayers": Martin Luther King Jr., "Letter from Birmingham Jail," Martin Luther King, Jr., and the Global Freedom Struggle, April 16, 1963, http://mlk-kpp01.stanford.edu/index.php/encyclopedia/documentsentry/annotated_letter_from_birmingham.

page 95   King was especially concerned: Stephen B. Oates, *Let the Trumpet Sound: The Life of Martin Luther King, Jr.* (New York: Harper & Row, 1982), p. 213.

page 95   On the Saturday before Easter: Martin Frady, *Martin Luther King, Jr.: A Life* (New York: Penguin, 2006), p. 106.

page 95   King pored over the statement: Carson, ed., *Autobiography*, p. 187.

page 96   "I suspect King was furious": Warren Goldstein, "Martin Luther King Jr. in Birmingham, Alabama," C-SPAN Video Library, November 15, 2011, www.c-spanvideo.org/program/302771-1.

page 96   As he attempted to reach a resolution: Carson, ed., *Autobiography*, p. 70.

page 97   He said he became so "upset": Ibid., p. 187.

CHAPTER 8: THE JAILHOUSE MANIFESTO

page 99   "if we mounted a strong nonviolent movement": Wyatt Tee Walker, quoted in Henry Hampton and Steve Fayer, *Voices of Freedom: An Oral History of the Civil Rights Movement from the 1950s Through the 1980s* (New York: Bantam Books, 1990), p. 125.

page 99   King grabbed a pen and began to write: Taylor Branch, *Parting the Waters: America in the King Years, 1954-1963* (New York: Simon & Schuster, 1988), p. 738.

page 100   Martin Luther King Jr.'s lawyer Clarence Jones: Clarence Jones, telephone interview with the author, February 17, 2012.

page 100   Coretta King, back home: Stewart Burns, *To the Mountaintop:*

Martin Luther King Jr.'s Mission to Save America 1955-1968 (New York: HarperSanFrancisco, 2004), p. 188.

page 101   Dora McDonald, King's personal secretary: S. Jonathan Bass, *Blessed Are the Peacemakers: Martin Luther King Jr., Eight White Religious Leaders, and the "Letter from Birmingham Jail"* (Baton Rouge: Louisiana State University Press, 2001), pp. 118-19.

page 101   Wyatt Walker received King's manifesto: Branch, *Parting the Waters*, p. 740.

page 103   "the movement that made Martin": Ella Baker, quoted in Kevin Boyle, "To the Mountaintop," *Chicago Tribune*, January 8, 2006, http://articles.chicagotribune.com/2006-01-08/entertainment/0601060386_1_king-years-martin-luther-king-stanley-levison.

page 104   Vernon Johns, who pastored: Branch, *Parting the Waters*, pp. 6-26.

page 104   "civil rights movement did not 'make' King": Richard Lischer, *The Preacher King: Martin Luther King Jr. and the Word That Moved America* (New York: Oxford University Press, 1995), p. 197.

page 104   prominent King contemporaries: Margalit Fox, "Dorothy Height, Largely Unsung Giant of the Civil Rights Era, Dies at 98," *New York Times*, April 20, 2010 www.nytimes.com/2010/04/21/us/21height.html?_r=0.

page 105   "I need your help": Branch, *Parting the Waters*, p. 185.

CHAPTER 9: "MY DEAR FELLOW CLERGYMEN"

Author's note: Among the sources that I found helpful for background and as a roadmap for this chapter were Paul T. Murray, "Martin Luther King, Jr.: "Letter from Birmingham Jail," Milestone Documents, www.milestonedocuments.com/documents/view/martin-luther-king-jrs-letter-from-birmingham-jail; and John J. Ansbro, *Martin Luther King, Jr.: The Making of a Mind* (Maryknoll, NY: Orbis, 1982).

page 107   "Letter from Birmingham Jail" marks a synthesis: S. Jonathan Bass, *Blessed Are the Peacemakers: Martin Luther King Jr., Eight White Religious Leaders, and the "Letter from Birmingham Jail"* (Baton Rouge: Louisiana State University Press, 2001), p. 116.

page 107 "King's conciliatory tone": Wesley T. Mott, "The Rhetoric of Martin Luther King, Jr.: Letter from Birmingham Jail," *Phylon* 36 (1975): 411-21.

page 108 "Power concedes nothing without a demand": Frederick Douglass, "West India Emancipation," August 3, 1857, quoted in "If There Is No Struggle, There Is No Progress," Blackpast.org, www.blackpast.org/?q=1857-frederick-douglass-if-there-no-struggle-there-no-progress.

page 111 "In a semiconscious way he may have been addressing": Stewart Burns, *To the Mountaintop: Martin Luther King Jr.'s Mission to Save America 1955-1968* (New York: HarperSan-Francisco, 2004), p. 185.

page 115 "Perhaps in a less emotional time": Bass, *Blessed Are the Peacemakers*, p. 2.

page 115 ministers believed the letter "cruel and unfair": Ibid., p. 149.

page 115 Earl Stallings, the Baptist minister: Ibid., p. 212.

page 115 Edward Ramage, the Presbyterian pastor: Ibid., pp. 209, 212.

page 115 Paul Hardin, the Methodist bishop: Ibid., p. 207.

page 115 George Murray, the Episcopalian bishop: Ibid., pp. 198-99.

page 116 Nolan Harmon, the other Methodist bishop: Ibid., pp. 164-65.

page 116 Charles Carpenter, another Episcopalian bishop: Ibid., p. 167.

page 116 Rabbi Milton Grafman described the letter: Ibid., pp. 176-77.

page 116 Joseph Durick saw the letter as: Ibid., p. 188.

page 118 "God's companionship does not stop": Martin Luther King Jr., *The Autobiography of Martin Luther King, Jr.*, ed. Clayborne Carson (New York: Warner Books 1998), p. 186.

CHAPTER 10: TAKING IT TO THE STREETS

page 119 Michael Wesley has observed a grit and decency: Michael Wesley, telephone interview with the author, February 4, 2013.

page 121 After eight days in the Birmingham Jail: Martin Frady, *Martin Luther King, Jr.: A Life* (New York: Penguin, 2006), p. 110.

page 121 "We've got to pick up everything": Martin Luther King Jr., quoted in ibid.

page 122 "Up to this point, about five to ten": James Bevel, quoted in

Henry Hampton and Steve Fayer, *Voices of Freedom: An Oral History of the Civil Rights Movement from the 1950s Through the 1980s* (New York: Bantam Books, 1990), p. 131.

page 122   King rejected Bevel's plan outright: Cynthia Levinson, *We've Got a Job: The 1963 Birmingham Children's March* (Atlanta: Peachtree Publishers, 2012), pp. 166-68.

page 123   Though he was still reluctant: Frady, *Martin Luther King, Jr.*, pp. 110-12.

page 123   Janice Kelsey's story: Janice Kelsey, telephone interview with the author, February 4, 2013.

page 126   Bull Connor lost whatever cool he had: Ira Peck, *The Life and Words of Martin Luther King, Jr.* (New York: Scholastic, 1968), pp. 60-61.

page 126   Rev. A. D. King leads a group of marchers: Cynthia Levinson, *We've Got a Job: The 1963 Birmingham Children's March* (Atlanta: Peachtree Publishers, 2012), p. 104.

page 126   Fred Burnett was an eighteen-year-old student: Curtiss Paul DeYoung, *Reconciliation: Our Greatest Challenge—Our Only Hope* (Valley Forge, PA: Judson Press, 1997), pp. 51-52. I am indebted to Curtiss Paul DeYoung for directing me to Burnett's story.

page 127   Bull Connor had played into the movement's hands: Peck, *Life and Words of Martin Luther King, Jr.*, pp. 60-61.

page 128   President Kennedy surveyed the turmoil: Harvard Sitkoff, *King: Pilgrimage to the Mountaintop* (New York: Hill & Wang, 2008), p. 112.

page 128   "An injured, maimed or dead child": Robert Kennedy, quoted in "Robert Kennedy Warns of 'Increasing Turmoil,'" *New York Times*, May 4, 1963, p. 8.

page 128   Kennedys dispatched Burke Marshall: Stewart Burns, *To the Mountaintop: Martin Luther King Jr.'s Mission to Save America 1955-1968* (New York: HarperSanFrancisco, 2004), p. 195.

page 128   Shuttlesworth provided adult leadership: Diane McWhorter, *Carry Me Home: Birmingham, Alabama—The Climatic Battle of the Civil Rights Revolution* (New York: Simon & Schuster, 2001), p. 405.

page 128   King worked hard to calm the fears: Taylor Branch, *Parting the Waters: America in the King Years, 1954-1963* (New York: Simon & Schuster, 1988), pp. 778-81.

page 129   "We agreed to call it off": Howell Raines, *My Soul Is Rested: The Story of the Civil Rights Movement in the Deep South* (New York: Penguin, 1983), pp. 159-61; McWhorter, *Carry Me Home*, pp. 414, 416-17.

page 130   concessions from the white leaders: Stephen B. Oates, *Let the Trumpet Sound: The Life of Martin Luther King, Jr.* (New York: Harper & Row, 1982), pp. 232-33.

page 130   The Chamber's deal with King: Diane McWhorter, interviewed by Frances Degen Horowitz on *Women to Women*, City University of New York, November 3, 2004, www.cuny.tv/show/womentowomen/PR1006431.

page 131   KKK had to have the final word: Sitkoff, *King*, p. 107.

page 131   the four little girls were killed: Charles E. Cobb Jr., *On the Road to Freedom: A Guided Tour of the Civil Rights Trail* (Chapel Hill, NC: Algonquin Books, 2008), p. 257.

page 131   Shuttlesworth recalled the devastation: Fred Shuttlesworth, quoted in Henry Hampton and Steve Fayer, *Voices of Freedom: An Oral History of the Civil Rights Movement from the 1950s Through the 1980s* (New York: Bantam Books, 1990), pp. 173-74.

page 132   Valley Forge or Gettysburg or Antietam: Warren Goldstein, "Martin Luther King Jr. in Birmingham, Alabama," C-SPAN Video Library, November 15, 2011, www.c-spanvideo.org/program/302771-1.

page 132   "I was upset with Dr. King": David Vann interview, *Eyes on the Prize Interviews*, November 1, 1985, Washington University Digital Gateway Texts, http://digital.wustl.edu/e/eop/eopweb/van0015.0251.102davidjvann.html.

page 133   "perfected the arts of delay and denial": Scott L. Malcolmson, *One Drop of Blood: The American Misadventure of Race* (New York: Farrar, Straus & Giroux, 2000), pp. 246-50.

pages 133-34 1963 "Man of the Year": David J. Garrow, *Bearing the Cross: Martin Luther King, Jr. and the Southern Christian Leadership Conference* (London: Vintage, 1986), p. 309.

page 134   "There are years that ask questions": Zora Neale Hurston,

Their Eyes Were Watching God (Champaign: University of Illinois Press, 1991), p. 27.

CHAPTER 11: DREAMS AND NIGHTMARES

page 135   "Return of the King": Aaron McGruder et al., "Return of the King," *The Boondocks*, season 1, episode 9, January 15, 2006, www.imdb.com/title/tt0757389.

page 137   civil rights activists came down hard: See "Sharpton Criticizes 'Boondocks' for Showing King Saying the N-Word," *USA Today*, January 25, 2006, http://usatoday30.usatoday.com/life/television/news/2006-01-25-sharpton-boondocks_x.htm.

page 137   "I was a new teacher": Jennifer Parker, email interview with the author, July 17, 2012.

page 139   "It's easy to forget how despised": Debra Dean Murphy, email interview with the author, July 10, 2012.

page 140   "struggles with depression and insomnia": Taylor Branch, *At Canaan's Edge: America in the King Years, 1965-68* (New York: Simon & Schuster, 2006), p. 216.

page 140   massive Poor People's Campaign: Edward Gilbreath, "Catching Up with a Dream," *Christianity Today*, March 2, 1998, www.ctlibrary.com/ct/1998/march2/8t3020.html.

page 140   1958 incident in Harlem: Stephen B. Oates, *Let the Trumpet Sound: The Life of Martin Luther King, Jr.* (New York: Harper & Row, 1982), pp. 134-35.

page 140   "This is a sick": Harvard Sitkoff, *King: Pilgrimage to the Mountaintop* (New York: Hill & Wang, 2008), p. 129.

page 140   In the late 90s: Andrew Young, interview with the author, University of Chicago, April 24, 1995.

page 141   "the grimmest look on his face": James Earl Massey, quoted in Gilbreath, "Catching Up with a Dream."

pages 141-42   He had "been to the mountaintop": Martin Luther King Jr., "I See the Promised Land," in *A Testament of Hope: The Essential Writings and Speeches of Martin Luther King*, ed. James M. Washington (San Francisco: HarperSanFrancisco, 1986), pp. 279-86.

page 142   "Whites, it must frankly be said": King, quoted in ibid., p. 561.

page 142   "a real Christian": See Steven Hayward, "Martin Luther

King, Conservative?" *Free Republic*, January 21, 2013, www.freerepublic.com/focus/f-news/2980539/posts.

page 143   a sermon King had planned: Jon Meacham and Vern E. Smith, "The War Over King's Legacy," *Newsweek*, April 6, 1998, www.washingtonpost.com/wp-srv/national/longterm/mlk/legacy/legacy.htm.

page 143   "Their graders were horrible": Jerald January, in discussion with the author, June 12, 2012.

CHAPTER 12: AFTER THE REVOLUTION

page 146   "I guess that's Birmingham down below": Stephen B. Oates, *Let the Trumpet Sound: The Life of Martin Luther King, Jr.* (New York: Harper & Row, 1982), p. 271.

page 147   "Things are better here today": Tracy Hipps, telephone interview with the author, January 28, 2013. For more on Christian Service Mission, see http://csmission.org.

page 150   "one of the nation's most livable cities": City of Birmingham website, www.informationbirmingham.com/about-birmingham.aspx.

page 150   "our history makes it stand out": Kevin Moore, telephone interview with the author, January 29, 2013.

page 151   "The challenge is with the municipal governments": Michael Wesley, telephone interview with the author, February 4, 2013.

page 154   What historian Warren Goldstein likes: Warren Goldstein, "Martin Luther King Jr. in Birmingham, Alabama," C-SPAN Video Library, November 15, 2011, www.c-spanvideo.org/program/302771-1.

page 154   unusual homage to the city's legacy: See the Birmingham Pledge, www.birminghampledge.org/about.html.

page 155   "There's a rush to closure": Diane McWhorter, speech at the Rotaract Club of Birmingham, April 7, 2011, www.youtube.com/watch?v=673tDuXsQ6A&feature=endscreen&NR=1.

CHAPTER 13: KING AMONG THE EVANGELICALS

page 156   William Pannell cannot recall: William Pannell, interview and emails with the author, February 1, 2013.

page 156   Learned bishops sat with lay evangelists: James Earl Massey, *Concerning Christian Unity: A Study of the Relational Imperative of Agape Love* (Prestonburg, KY: Reformation Publishers, 1979). Chapter eleven, "Concerning Christian Unity," available online at *Messages from the Heart*, www.heart-talks.com/christianunityc .html.

page 158   "Folks in my church": Philip Yancey, *Soul Survivor: How My Faith Survived the Church* (New York: Doubleday, 2001), p. 17.

page 159   "It was not until": Edward J. Blum, email interview with the author, July 10, 2013.

page 159   Glen Kehrein shared with me: Edward Gilbreath, "Catching Up with a Dream," *Christianity Today*, March 2, 1998, www .ctlibrary.com/ct/1998/march2/8t3020.html.

page 161   He wrestled with feelings of guilt: Taylor Branch, *Parting the Waters: America in the King Years, 1954-1963* (New York: Simon & Schuster, 1988), pp. 677-79.

page 161   King's struggles with despondency: Stephen B. Oates, *Let the Trumpet Sound: The Life of Martin Luther King, Jr.* (New York: Harper & Row, 1982), pp. 273-75.

page 162   "It was precisely in King's humanness": Debra Dean Murphy, email interview with the author, July 10, 2012.

page 162   "The religion of King and his associates": Mark A. Noll, *God and Race in American Politics: A Short History* (Princeton, NJ: Princeton University Press, 2008), p. 108.

page 162   King as a theological resource among evangelicals: Peter Goodwin Heltzel, *Jesus and Justice: Evangelicals, Race, and American Politics* (New Haven, CT: Yale University Press, 2009), pp. 45-47.

page 163   "the arc of the moral universe": A phrase often sampled by Dr. King in his speeches, most notably during his message at the conclusion of the Selma-to-Montgomery march on March 25, 1965.

EPILOGUE

page 164   black theology conference in August 1979: Kenneth A. Briggs, "Black Theologians Want to Add a Letter by Dr. King to the Bible," *New York Times*, August 5, 1979, p. 42.

page 164   South Africa's anti-apartheid movement: Douglas Brinkley, "Martin Luther King's 'Letter from Birmingham Jail,'" *American History*, August 2003, http://iipdigital.usembassy .gov/st/english/article/2007/02/20070205165927eaifas 0.9735529.html#ixzz2LMa4InKJ.

page 165   "Many of us who do speaking and training": Joel Pérez, telephone interview the author, February 5, 2013.

page 165   "I'm a lifelong Republican": Carl Ruby, email and telephone interviews with the author, July 11, 2012.

page 168   "what made me act the fool": Fred Shuttlesworth, quoted in *Birmingham's Revolutionary: The Reverend Fred Shuttlesworth and the Alabama Christian Movement for Human Rights*, ed. Marjorie L. White and Andrew M. Manis (Macon, GA: Mercer University Press, 2000), p. 77.

page 169   As one biographer put it: Martin Frady, *Martin Luther King, Jr.: A Life* (New York: Penguin, 2006), p. 109.

page 169   "It is easier to write ten volumes": Leo Tolstoy, *The Diaries of Leo Tolstoy: Youth, 1847-1852*, entry dated March 17, 1846 or 1847, trans. C. J. Hogarth and A. Sirnis (New York: E. P. Dutton, 1917), p. 2.

Recommended Reading on Race, MLK and the Civil Rights Movement

Baldwin, Lewis V. *Never to Leave Us Alone: The Prayer Life of Martin Luther King Jr.* Minneapolis: Fortress Press, 2010.

———. *There Is a Balm in Gilead: The Cultural Roots of Martin Luther King Jr.* Minneapolis: Augsburg Fortress, 1991.

Bass, S. Jonathan. *Blessed Are the Peacemakers: Martin Luther King Jr., Eight White Religious Leaders, and the "Letter from Birmingham Jail."* Baton Rouge: Louisiana State University Press, 2001.

Branch, Taylor. *At Canaan's Edge: America in the King Years, 1965-68.* New York: Simon & Schuster, 2006.

———. *Parting the Waters: America in the King Years, 1954-63.* New York: Simon & Schuster, 1988.

———. *Pillar of Fire: America in the King Years, 1963-65.* New York: Simon & Schuster, 1998.

Burns, Stewart. *To the Mountaintop: Martin Luther King Jr.'s Mission to Save America 1955-1968.* New York: HarperSanFrancisco, 2004.

Burrow, Rufus, Jr. *Martin Luther King Jr. for Armchair Theologians.* Louisville, KY: Westminster John Knox, 2009.

Carson, Clayborne, ed. *The Autobiography of Martin Luther King Jr.* New York: Warner Books, 1998.

———, ed. *The Papers of Martin Luther King Jr.* Vols. 1-6. Berkeley: University of California Press, 1992, 1994, 1997, 2000, 2005, 2007.

Carson, Clayborne, and Peter Holloran, eds. *A Knock at Midnight: Inspiration from the Great Sermons of Reverend Martin Luther King, Jr.* New York: Warner Books, 1998.

Cobb, Charles E., Jr. *On the Road to Freedom: A Guided Tour of the Civil Rights Trail.* Chapel Hill, NC: Algonquin Books, 2008.

Colaiaco, James A. Martin *Luther King Jr.: Apostle of Militant Nonviolence.* New York: Saint Martin's Press, 1993.

DeYoung, Curtiss Paul. *Living Faith: How Faith Inspires Social Justice.* Minneapolis: Fortress Press, 2007.

Dyson, Michael Eric. *I May Not Get There with You: The True Martin Luther King Jr.* New York: Free Press, 2000.

Eskew, Glenn T. *But for Birmingham: The Local and National Movements in the Civil Rights Struggle.* Chapel Hill: University of North Carolina Press, 1997.

Fairclough, Adam. *Better Day Coming: Blacks and Equality, 1890-2000.* New York: Penguin, 2001.

———. *Martin Luther King Jr.* Athens: University of Georgia Press, 1995.

———. *To Redeem the Soul of America: The Southern Christian Leadership Conference and Martin Luther King Jr.* Athens: University of Georgia Press, 1987.

Frady, Marshall. *Martin Luther King, Jr.: A Life.* New York: Penguin, 2002.

Garrow, David J. *Bearing the Cross: Martin Luther King, Jr., and the Southern Christian Leadership Conference.* London: Vintage, 1986.

Hampton, Henry, and Steve Fayer. *Voices of Freedom: An Oral History of the Civil Rights Movement from the 1950s Through the 1980s.* New York: Bantam Books, 1990.

Hansen, Drew D. *The Dream: Martin Luther King Jr. and the Speech That Inspired a Nation.* New York: Ecco/HarperCollins, 2003.

Harding, Vincent. *Martin Luther King: The Inconvenient Hero.* Rev. ed. Maryknoll, NY: Orbis, 2008.

Heltzel, Peter Goodwin. *Jesus and Justice: Evangelicals, Race, and American Politics.* New Haven, CT: Yale University Press, 2009.

Jackson, Troy. *Becoming King: Martin Luther King Jr. and the Making of a National Leader.* Lexington: University Press of Kentucky, 2008.

Jenkins, Willis, and Jennifer M. McBride, eds. *Bonhoeffer and King:*

Their Legacies and Import for Christian Social Thought. Minneapolis: Fortress Press, 2010.

Jones, Clarence B., and Joel Engel. *What Would Martin Say?* New York: HarperCollins, 2008.

Jones, Clarence B., and Stuart Connelly. *Behind the Dream: The Making of the Speech That Transformed a Nation.* New York: Palgrave Macmillan, 2011.

Lischer, Richard. *The Preacher King: Martin Luther King Jr. and the Word That Moved America.* New York: Oxford University Press, 1995.

Manis, Andrew M. *A Fire You Can't Put Out: The Civil Rights Life of Birmingham's Reverend Fred Shuttlesworth.* Tuscaloosa: University of Alabama Press, 1999.

Marsh, Charles. *The Beloved Community: How Faith Shapes Social Justice, from the Civil Rights Movement to Today.* New York: Basic Books, 2004.

———. *God's Long Summer: Stories of Faith and Civil Rights.* Princeton, NJ: Princeton University Press, 1997.

McWhorter, Diane. *Carry Me Home: Birmingham, Alabama—the Climatic Battle of the Civil Rights Revolution.* New York: Simon & Schuster, 2001.

Noll, Mark A. *God and Race in American Politics: A Short History.* Princeton, NJ: Princeton University Press, 2008.

Oates, Stephen B. *Let the Trumpet Sound: The Life of Martin Luther King, Jr.* New York: Harper & Row, 1982.

Rieder, Jonathan. *Gospel of Freedom: Martin Luther King Jr.'s Letter from Birmingham Jail and the Struggle that Changed a Nation.* New York: Bloomsbury Press, 2013.

———. *The Word of The Lord Is Upon Me: The Righteous Performance of Martin Luther King Jr.* Cambridge, MA: Belknap Press, 2008.

Roberts, J. Deotis. *Bonhoeffer & King: Speaking Truth to Power.* Louisville, KY: Westminster John Knox, 2005.

Roediger, David R. *How Race Survived U.S. History: From Settlement and Slavery to the Obama Phenomenon.* New York: Verso, 2008.

Sitkoff, Harvard. *King: Pilgrimage to the Mountaintop.* New York: Hill & Wang, 2008.

Warren, Mervyn A. *King Came Preaching: The Pulpit Power of Dr. Martin Luther King Jr.* Downers Grove, IL: InterVarsity Press, 2001.

Washington, James M., ed. *A Testament of Hope: The Essential Writings and Speeches of Martin Luther King, Jr.* San Francisco: HarperSan-Francisco, 1986.

Index

Abernathy, Ralph, 30, 47, 53, 60, 67, 70-71, 96, 121, 160-61
affirmative action, 14, 90
Alabama Christian Movement for Human Rights (ACMHR), 27, 65, 66
Albany, Georgia, 61-62, 66, 67, 69, 95, 121, 145
Ali, Muhammad, 10
All Saints' Church, Wittenberg, Germany, 9
Anderson University School of Theology, 126, 141
"Angry Black Man," 89
Anniston, Alabama, 60
Appalachian Mountains, 146, 148, 150
Aristotle, 38
Arlington, Texas, 73
Atlanta, Georgia, 21, 32, 42-44, 57, 59, 92, 108, 146, 151
    MLK's childhood in, 32, 33
    Sweet Auburn district in, 32, 34
Augustine, Saint, 18, 38, 109, 114, 166
Avengers, The, 88
Azbell, Joe, 50
Baker, Ella, 53, 58, 103-4
Baldwin, Lewis, 52
Bass, S. Jonathan, 83-84, 86, 115
Belafonte, Harry, 93, 102
Bell, Ralph, 157
Bell, William, 147, 152
beloved community, 15, 139
Bentham, Jeremy, 38
Bethel Baptist Church (Birmingham), 25, 28, 66
Bevel, James, 122-25
Billy Graham Evangelistic Association (BGEA), 156
Birmingham, Alabama, 15, 60, 62, 64, 108, 145, 146-47, 163
    "Big Mules" in, 21
    as "Bombingham," 22

Children's Crusade in, 122-23, 126-27, 168
division among blacks in, 64-65
Dynamite Hill in, 22
Freedom Rides in, 60, 63, 65
and Great Depression, 24
importance of black churches in, 23-24
as industrial center, 21, 31
as "Magic City," 21
origins of, 21-22
as "Pittsburgh of the South," 150
police in, 15, 112
political structure in, 65-66, 151
Project C in, 68, 79, 82, 95
racial reconciliation and, 17
racism in, 15, 60, 64, 150-51
Red Mountain as a barrier in, 148
and results of MLK's campaign in, 133
urban-suburban division in, 151-53
Warren G. Harding in, 21
Birmingham Civil Rights Institute, 63, 146, 148, 165
Birmingham Eight (white clergymen)
    Carpenter, Charles Colcock Jones (Episcopalian), 81, 85, 106, 116
    Durick, Joseph A. (Catholic), 81, 84, 85, 106, 116
    Good Friday Statement of, 80-82, 83
    Grafman, Milton L. (Jewish), 82, 84, 85, 106, 116

Hardin, Paul (Methodist), 82, 85, 106, 115
Harmon, Nolan B. (Methodist), 82, 85, 106, 116
    and "Letter from Birmingham Jail," 87, 106, 115
Murray, George M. (Episcopalian), 82, 85, 106, 115
Ramage, Edward V. (Presbyterian), 82, 86, 106, 115
    risks and personal costs of, 84-85
Stallings, Earl (Baptist), 82, 86, 106, 111, 115, 117
    and their opposition to MLK in Birmingham, 79-82, 106, 113-15
Birmingham News, 77, 95, 99, 101
"Birmingham Pledge, The," 154-55
Birmingham Post-Herald, 64
Birmingham World, 78
Birmingham-Easonian Baptist Bible College, 23
Black Muslims (Nation of Islam), 110, 139
Blessed Are the Peacemakers (Bass), 83
Blum, Edward, 159
Boondocks, The, 135-37
Boston University, 38, 40
Boutwell, Albert, 66, 77, 80, 107, 132
Bradley, Sarah (Mrs. Bradley), 92
Bridges, Eleanor, 64
Brightman, Edgar S., 39
Brown v. Board of Education, 11, 13, 29, 47, 109, 114
Buber, Martin, 168
Burnett, Fred, 126
Burns, Stewart, 110-11

Calvinists, 84

Carlyle, Thomas, 32

Carry Me Home (McWhorter), 130

Cartoon Network, 135

Catholic Church, 9-10

CBS, 63

Cedarville University, 165-67

Charlotte, North Carolina, 151

Chicago, Illinois, 18, 23, 43, 44, 74, 132, 139, 156, 160

Christian Service Mission (Birmingham), 147, 149

Church of God in Christ, 141

Cincinnati, Ohio, 66

Circle Urban Ministries (Chicago), 160

Civil Rights Act of 1964, 14, 133

Civil War, 13, 32, 47, 104

Colorado Springs, Colorado, 143

Colvin, Claudette, 47

Congress of Racial Equality (CORE), 59, 104

Connor, Eugene "Bull," 22, 28, 60, 65-66, 77, 107, 131, 155, 168
    Birmingham campaign and, 69, 71, 100, 112, 122, 126-27, 147
    Freedom Rides and, 60, 65

Cotton, Dorothy, 70

Crozer Theological Seminary (Pennsylvania), 37, 38-39

DeMille, Cecil B., 95

Democrats, 128, 133

Denver, Colorado, 143

Detroit, Michigan, 19, 132

DeWolf, L. Harold, 39

Dexter Avenue Baptist Church (Montgomery), 40-41, 46, 57, 104

Douglass, Frederick, 12, 18, 104, 108, 168

Dublin, Georgia, 92

Du Bois, W. E. B., 11, 12, 33, 104
    and concept of race, 11
    "double consciousness" theme of, 76

Duke Divinity School, 38

Dunbar, Paul Laurence, 89

Ebenezer Baptist Church (Atlanta), 33, 41, 57

Eliot, T. S., 18, 112

Ellwanger, Joseph, 77

Emancipation Proclamation, 13

Evangelical Free Church of America, 16

evangelicals (and evangelical movement), 55, 72, 76, 98, 156-58

Evers, Medgar, 134

Facebook, 29, 98

Fallin, Wilson, Jr., 23-24

Farmer, James, 104

First Baptist Church of Montgomery, 30, 47

Fisk University, 58

Fox News, 90

Freedom Riders, 59-61, 65

Fuller Theological Seminary, 156

Gandhi, Mohandas, 37

Gaston, Arthur (A. G.), 65, 78, 79, 122

Gaston Motel (Birmingham), 70-71, 79, 83, 102, 131, 146

George Fox Evangelical Seminary, 54

Gladstone, William, 114

Goldberg, Michelle, 90

Goldstein, Warren, 96, 154

Graetz, Robert, 49-50, 77

Graham, Billy, 16, 48, 77, 78, 107

Graves, John Temple, 64

Great Migration, 19-21

Greater Shiloh Baptist Church (Birmingham), 22, 119, 133, 149

Greensboro, North Carolina, 57

Hammond, Wizdom Powell, 89

Harding, Warren G., 21-22

Height, Dorothy, 104

Heltzel, Peter, 162-63

Heschel, Abraham Joshua, 77

Hipps, Tracy, 147-51

Hobbes, Thomas, 38

Holt Street Baptist Church (Montgomery), 29, 47

Huntsville, Alabama, 20

Hurston, Zora Neale, 134

"I Have a Dream" speech, 10, 16, 56, 87, 139-40, 145, 159, 167

immigration (and illegal immigration), 14, 45, 90
    African Americans and, 19, 20
    and reform, 165, 166-67

integration, 13, 16, 22, 52, 70, 86, 109, 116, 148

Jackson, Emory O., 78

Jackson, Jesse, 89, 160

Jackson, Mississippi, 137, 159

Jackson, Troy, 47

Jacksonville, Florida, 151

January, Jerald, 74-76, 143-45

Jefferson, Thomas, 110, 168

Jesus (and Christ), 51, 52, 110, 122, 145, 158, 166-69

Jesus and Justice (Heltzel), 162

Jim Crow (laws), 13, 19, 20, 22, 45, 47, 52, 68, 91, 93, 109, 155

John Henry, 10

Johns, Vernon, 104

Johnson, Lyndon B., 133

Johnson, Mordecai, 37

Jones, Clarence B., 99-103

Jones, Howard O., 156-57

Kehrein, Glen, 159-61

Kelly Ingram Park (Birmingham), 125-26, 131, 147, 154

Kelsey, George, 37

Kelsey, Janice (Wesley), 121, 123-26, 132-33

Kennedy, John F. (JFK), 59, 78, 107, 128-29, 131, 133, 134

Kennedy, Robert F. (RFK), 59, 60, 78, 107, 128

King, A. D. (MLK's brother), 34, 126, 131

King, Alberta Williams (MLK's mother), 33, 34

King Center, The, 144

King, Christine (MLK's sister), 34

King, Coretta Scott (MLK's wife), 36, 40, 41, 48, 59, 95, 100, 140, 161

King, Martin Luther, Jr. (MLK)
  and accusations of communism, 160-61
  on America's racism, 12
  anger and frustration of, 91-92, 93, 94, 95-97, 109
  arrests of, 58, 71
  assassination of, 141-42
  on being an "extremist," 110-11
  on the beloved community, 15
  and Birmingham campaign, 68-71, 121-23, 128-29
  and Birmingham Eight, 82-84, 95, 113-17
  in Birmingham Jail, 15, 71, 94-97, 98-99, 100-102, 121
  black critics of, 58, 78, 107
  black preaching disliked by, 35
  bombing of home of, 49, 140
  call of, 40, 55-56
  cautious personality of, 31-32, 67, 93, 102
  in Chicago, 18, 139
  and Christian discipleship, 16, 17
  Christian upbringing of, 38
  chronic exhaustion of, 105, 140
  on the church, 16, 112, 158
  and civil rights forerunners, 103-4
  contrasted with Shuttlesworth, 31
  as copastor at Ebenezer Baptist, 57
  and courtship of Coretta Scott, 36
  death threats and physical attacks experienced by, 91, 140

  depression of, 140
  and disagreements with Shuttlesworth, 67, 129
  doubts and anxieties of, 51, 67, 105, 140
  early life of, 33-35
  education of, 35-40, 169
  and evangelicals, 157-63
  extramarital affairs of, 159, 161, 162
  and failure in Albany, 61-62, 66, 67, 95, 121
  and first encounters with racism, 34-35, 92
  as a folk hero, 10, 93-94
  and Freedom Riders, 60
  Gandhi's influence on, 37, 52
  genius of, 14, 87, 103, 105, 168-69
  in Germany, 157
  and "Give Us the Ballot" speech, 56-57
  growing prominence of, 56, 58, 104
  holiday in honor of, 137, 161
  and "I Have a Dream" speech, 10, 56, 139, 145, 167
  as imagined in *The Boondocks*, 135-37
  and impatience with white Christians, 101, 102, 111-12
  and interracial friendships, 36, 49, 77
  and JFK, 59, 78, 100, 107, 129, 140
  liberal theology of, 38-39, 162
  mentors in life of, 37
  and the Montgomery boycott, 48-52, 55, 96, 98
  as "Moses" of civil rights, 14, 56
  and "Mountaintop" speech, 18, 141-42
  name change of, 33, 34
  on Native Americans, 12
  and Nobel Peace Prize, 133

  nonviolence philosophy of, 14, 52, 66, 93, 94, 99
  opposition to Birmingham presence of, 77, 79, 106
  and opposition to Vietnam War, 18, 139
  as pastor of Dexter Avenue Baptist, 40-41, 46, 57
  physical appearance of, 18, 36
  plagiarism of, 39, 161, 169
  and Poor People's Campaign, 140
  prayer in life of, 40, 48, 50, 51-52, 70, 95, 118, 161, 167, 169
  preaching of, 41, 46, 49, 140
  as prophet, 10, 91, 93
  revisionist history of, 93-94, 139, 143
  SCLC leadership of, 52-53, 56, 67
  SNCC criticism of, 58
  and sit-in movement, 57-58, 59
  and the Social Gospel, 38-39
  struggles with guilt by, 57, 96, 161, 169
  and support of Memphis sanitation workers, 140
  as a symbol, 76, 105
  as *Time*'s "Man of the Year," 133
  and use of media, 76-77, 98-99, 117, 155
  "vision in the kitchen" of, 51

King, Martin Luther, Sr. (Daddy King), 33-34, 39, 41, 51, 69

King, Yolanda (MLK's daughter), 51

Ku Klux Klan, 22, 28, 50, 60, 65, 66, 70, 109, 112, 130-31

Lawson, James, 58

Lee, Spike, 89

Lemann, Nicholas, 19
"Letter from Birmingham Jail,"
    10, 16-17, 55, 87, 106, 139
    as expression of MLK's
        anger, 96-97, 102, 107
    on extremism, 110-11
    and MLK's evolution,
        18, 107, 111
    and MLK on "just laws,"
        109, 114, 165
    publication of, 121
    proposal for
        canonization of, 164
    as used by international
        movements, 164
    on white moderates, 109
Levison, Stanley, 77, 100
Lewis, John, 58, 104
Lincoln, Abraham, 13, 104,
    110
Lischer, Richard, 38, 39, 104
Locke, John, 38
Los Angeles, California,
    100, 146
Lowery, Joseph, 53
Lucy, Autherine, 26
Luter, Fred, 73
Luther, Martin, 9-10, 18, 33,
    98, 110
Mackey, Willie Pearl, 101
Malcolm X, 139
Mandela, Nelson, 164
Manis, Andrew, 28, 67
Marley, Bob, 164
Marshall, Burke, 128-29
Martin, Trayvon, 45
Mason Temple (Memphis),
    141
Massey, James Earl, 141,
    156-57
Mays, Benjamin, 37
McDonald, Dora, 101
McGruder, Aaron, 135
McKissic, Dwight, 73
McWhorter, Diane, 24,
    130-31, 155
Memphis, Tennessee, 140-42
Meredith, James, 112
Mill, John Stuart, 38
Mission Birmingham, 150
Mobile, Alabama, 25, 29, 53, 81
Montgomery, Alabama,
    46-53, 56, 98, 127, 145

bus boycott in, 15, 29,
    47-49, 51
as capital of
    Confederacy, 47
Freedom Rides in, 60
MLK's first pastorate in,
    40-41, 46, 57
Montgomery Improvement
    Association (MIA), 29, 47,
    48, 98
Moody Bible Institute, 160
Moore, Kevin, 150-53
Morehouse College, 31, 35,
    38, 42
Mott, Wesley T., 107
Murphy, Debra Dean, 139,
    142-43, 162
My Friend, the Enemy
    (Pannell), 157
Nash, Diane, 58
Nashville, Tennessee, 58,
    120, 151
National Association for the
    Advancement of Colored
    People (NAACP), 24-25,
    26, 27, 46, 61, 104, 134
National Council of Negro
    Women, 104
National Urban League, 104
Native Americans, 12, 54
Neuhaus, Richard John, 77
New England Conservatory
    of Music, 36
New Orleans, Louisiana, 20
New York, New York, 132
New York Theological
    Seminary, 162
New York Times, 63, 73
Newsweek magazine, 77
Niebuhr, Reinhold, 18, 39,
    108
Ninety-Five Theses (Luther), 9
Nixon, E. D., 47
North Carolina A & T
    University, 57
NPR, 73
Obama, Barack, 11, 142
Offenburger, Tom, 77
"On Civil Disobedience"
    (Thoreau), 37
Pannell, William, 156-57
Park, Julie J., 17
Parker, Jennifer, 137-38

Parks, Rosa, 42, 45, 46-47, 75
Paul, the apostle, 102, 106,
    107, 110, 115, 166, 168
Pérez, Joel, 165
Phillips High School
    (Birmingham), 28
Plato, 38
Pritchett, Laurie, 61-62, 69
Promised Land, The
    (Lemann), 19
race
    and Christianity, 10, 13
    and "everyday racism,"
        89
    and racial profiling, 45
    and racialization, 12
    and reverse racism, 90
    and sin, 14, 64, 159
    as social construct, 11, 12
    theology of, 12, 14
Ramsay High School
    (Birmingham), 119
Randolph, A. Philip, 104
Rauschenbusch, Walter, 39
reconciliation (and racial
    reconciliation), 15, 16, 17,
    73, 76, 77, 87, 99, 115, 149,
    154, 166, 169
Reconciliation Blues
    (Gilbreath), 74, 75
Red Mountain
    (Birmingham), 147, 150
Republicans, 21, 165-66
Revelation Missionary
    Baptist Church
    (Cincinnati), 66
Rockefeller, Nelson, 102
Rockford, IL, 20
Rotch, James, 154
Rousseau, 38
Ruby, Carl, 165-67
Rustin, Bayard, 53
Salisbury, Harrison, 63-64
Samford University
    (Birmingham), 120
San Francisco, California, 132
Sanders, Alvin, 16
school desegregation, 13, 119
Seattle Pacific University, 165
Selma, Alabama, 18, 127,
    133
Shades Mountain Baptist
    Church (Birmingham), 149

Shores, Arthur, 26
Shuttlesworth, Fred L., 17,
  29, 42, 64, 65, 104,
  122-23, 128, 153
  and the Alabama
    Christian Movement
    for Human Rights, 27,
    65, 66
  background of, 25-26
  beat up by white mob, 28
  Bethel Baptist departure
    of, 66
  Birmingham airport
    named in honor of,
    146
  bombing of parsonage
    of, 28
  complicated
    relationship with
    MLK, 30, 129
  contrasted with MLK, 31
  death of, 168
  disagreements with
    MLK, 67, 129
  faith and activism of,
    26-27, 31, 67, 79, 129,
    168
  as founding member of
    SCLC, 53, 67
  and the Freedom Rides,
    61
  as member of NAACP, 26
  as pastor of Bethel
    Baptist, 26
  pastorate in Cincinnati
    of, 66
  preaching style of, 26
  as principal advocate for
    launch of Birmingham
    campaign, 67-68, 111
  on the Sixteenth Street
    Baptist bombing, 131
  and support of
    Montgomery
    campaign, 29
sit-ins, 57-59, 61, 62, 114
Sixteenth Street Baptist
  Church (Birmingham), 71,
  123, 124, 128, 165
  bombing of, 131, 133, 147
slavery in American history,
  13, 19, 21
Smith, Howard K., 63

Social Gospel movement,
  39, 84
Socrates, 18, 168
Soul Survivor (Yancey), 158
Southern Baptist
  Convention (SBC), 73
Southern Christian
  Leadership Conference
  (SCLC), 52, 56, 58, 60, 61,
  67, 78, 96, 99, 125, 140, 147
  failure in Albany of,
    61-62
  formation of, 52-53
  after MLK's death, 160
  MLK's national platform
    with, 57
  MLK's relationship with
    ministers of, 141
  and Project C in
    Birmingham, 68-69,
    95, 101, 102, 122, 128,
    130, 134
Spelman College, 36
Stanford University, 103
Steele, C. K., 53
Stride Toward Freedom
  (King), 49
Student Nonviolent
  Coordinating Committee
  (SNCC), 58, 59, 61, 104,
  111
Tallahassee, Florida, 53
Tennessee State University
  (Nashville), 120
*Their Eyes Were Watching
  God* (Hurston), 134
Thomas Aquinas, Saint, 18,
  38, 109, 166, 168
Thoreau, Henry David, 37,
  52, 107
Till, Emmett, 23
Time magazine, 77, 133, 146
Tolstoy, Leo, 169
Trinity Lutheran Church
  (Montgomery), 49
Twitter, 29, 98
Tyson, Tim, 94
Ullman High School
  (Birmingham), 123-24
University of Alabama
  (Tuscaloosa), 26
University of Mississippi
  (Oxford), 112

University of North
  Carolina (Chapel Hill), 89
Vann, David, 132
Vernon Park Church of God,
  74
Vietnam War, 18, 139
Voting Rights Act of 1965,
  14, 133
Walker, Wyatt Tee, 68, 99,
  101-2
Wallace, George, 79, 127
Warmth of Other Suns, The
  (Wilkerson), 19
Washington, Booker T., 12,
  33, 56, 104
Washington, D.C., 128, 140
  March on (1963), 56,
    133
  Prayer Pilgrimage in
    (1957), 56
Washington Post, 77
Way Out of No Way, A
  (Young), 141
"We Shall Overcome," 70, 125
Wesley, Alvin, 121, 126
Wesley, Michael W., 22-23,
  119, 149, 151-52
West, Cornel, 93
West Virginia Wesleyan
  College, 139
Where Do We Go from Here?
  (King), 142
Who Speaks for Birmingham?,
  63-64
Why We Can't Wait (King),
  78, 121
Wilkerson, Isabel, 19
Wilkins, Roy, 104
Williams, A. D. (MLK's
  grandfather), 33
Wood, Danny, 149
Woodlawn High School
  (Birmingham), 120
Woodley, Randy, 54
World Congress on
  Evangelism, 156-57
Wright, Jeremiah, 89, 142
Yancey, Philip, 39, 158
Young, Andrew, 125, 128,
  140-41
Young, Whitney, 104
Youth for Christ, 156

ABOUT THE AUTHOR

Edward Gilbreath is the author of *Reconciliation Blues: A Black Evangelical's Inside View of White Christianity*. An award-winning journalist, he serves as an editor at large for *Christianity Today* magazine and as the executive director of communications for the Evangelical Covenant Church.

Since the release of *Reconciliation Blues*, Ed has spoken to thousands of people across the nation at churches, conferences and university campuses on issues of race, faith and culture. He earned his bachelor's in communication arts from Judson University and a master's in philosophy of history from Olivet Nazarene University. He lives in the Chicago area with his wife, Dana, and their two children.

Visit Ed's website at www.edgilbreath.com.

BOOK DISCUSSION GUIDE AVAILABLE

Visit www.ivpress.com to download a group discussion guide for *Birmingham Revolution*.